CHURCH PLANNING AND MANAGEMENT

A Guide for Pastors and Laymen

by
B. OTTO WHEELEY
with
Thomas H. Cable

DORRANCE & COMPANY

Philadelphia

Contents

Preface

The Perfect Church

I think that I shall never see
A church that's all it ought to be;
A church whose members never stray
Beyond the straight and narrow way;
A church that has no empty pews,
Whose pastor never has the blues;
A church whose deacons always deak,
And none are proud and all are meek,
Where gossips never peddle lies,
Or make complaints or criticize;
Where all are always sweet and kind,
And all to others faults are blind.
Such perfect churches there may be,
But none of them is known to me,
But still I'll work and pray and plan
To make our own the best I can.

Anonymous

The author and his co-writer are essentially industrial executives who found in the course of their business lives the reality of God's power here on earth to change men's lives and to provide through prayer and faith in that power the answers to problems beyond their own ability to solve. They believe that some of the management methods and principles used in industry offer needed help for the church in today's crisis—and they have church experience to prove it.

Never before in America has there been such a need for Christ's church. And never before has the running of His church so badly needed expert management and operation. Yet the methods are helter-skelter. Why?

By the admission of pastors in various Protestant denominations, they are not trained in management methods either at the seminary or later through appropriate seminars. Also, students at the seminaries say they have no texts, no organized courses to help them in the area of management. On the few occasions where laymen with management experience speak to seminary students, they find hungry listeners and question-and-answer sessions that could go on all night.

Why this vacuum? The answer lies partly in the manner in which the Protestant church has evolved, with almost total emphasis on preaching, Bible reading, and prayer. These were fundamental and quite sufficient in the very early rural era and continue to be of basic importance. But with the urbanization of America, with its ever-increasing social complexity, these simplistic measures alone have not been enough to help the clergy effectively work through laity to keep the church in step with change and today's more baffling economic, social, and environmental problems.

For the church to retain or regain its central position in the community, it needs to avail itself of the methods used by other successful institutions (educational, business, and professional) to cope with the complexities within which these institutions not only survive, but fill leadership vacuums in community development. The church has lost its leadership role by default—not by conscious default, but by default nonetheless.

The restoration of this role has now become a long, hard road; but by embracing proven management methods which have been effective in other types of human endeavor, the church can expect a resurgence in its reaching, teaching, preaching role. The church has going for it the one great force which corporations and educational institutions are beginning to realize has been lacking in their approach to society—the spiritual side of man. Today, corporation managements are recognizing that employee satisfaction is waning —that higher and higher pay alone is not the answer. Employees are seeking to identify the worth of what they do in terms of its contribution to the quality of life. Employees ask the age-old

questions more and more—Who am I? Why am I here?—the same questions which have been the province of the church, but which are not being answered well enough by the church.

Pastor-Layman Roles

In offering this book, the authors believe that while the pastor's role is and must be preponderantly one of spiritual leadership, and that he comes into this role because God has singled him out to perform this special kind of ministry—nevertheless, he needs training in certain "enabling" arts and sciences to permit him to operate effectively in this role. Support for this thesis is found in God's choice of Paul to do His work. Had Paul not already had a practical background in the affairs of the day, his effectiveness could have been quite different.

Thus, it is believed that students in the seminaries must be given training in church management as well. Pastors who did not receive this must acquire it as an extra study on the job. The pastor's role as leader means that while he does not have to be an expert in every field of endeavor, he must have, as we say, expertise—he must know enough about each method or subject to manage it and to select and direct experts in each kind of endeavor. This means that he does not do all the actual work himself, as many try to do—and fail. But he must be able to select from the lay people persons who are experts and who can and will carry out the work of the church through the inspiration of the Holy Spirit. The lay people in the church have the role of carrying on all of the various tasks within a well-organized framework established and led by the pastor. Where the pastor knows or recognizes that he needs major help in organizing and managing, he should seek within the congregation, find, and put to work one who does have this talent and experience.

Why a Church Organization?

The scriptures teach that men are to assemble in fellowship and worship God (Heb. 10:24-25) and to perform services for their fellowmen. We have many descriptions and examples of the church

3

activities in both the Old and New Testaments, from Moses to Paul. Jethro, Moses' father-in-law (Exod. 18:13-27) was the author of modern management principles. He outlined to Moses how to institute an organization of people using "able men, such as fear God" to serve the people. In Acts 6:1-6, we see organization introduced to the "New Church" in the office of deacon ("full of spirit and wisdom") to serve the needs of the people, in this case, widows, who were being overlooked.

Many pastors may say, "I've got able men, but not spiritual men that truly love the Lord." If true, this clearly establishes a first priority—the development of a nucleus of such persons.

The church organization has its purpose in providing organization and facilities for worship, fellowship, Bible study, and various services which permit man to understand who he is and why he is here. And all these are essential in order to develop a sensitivity to God. To really understand the role of the church, we need to focus on man's basic makeup—physical, mental, and spiritual.

Millions of dollars and giant effort have been expended to prolong man's physical well-being—and with continuing success. More billions are spent to cram his head with knowledge, and more billions on leisure activities to benefit both his physical and mental processes. But what about the spiritual side—why has this not been given more recognition in our society? If, as many agree, man's eternal good and short-term wisdom come from God and are gained through spiritual development, why should not more time and money be spent for this purpose? Man's physical and mental development has outrun his spiritual development. And what is the church's role?

The church is the one institution (outside the family) that claims to serve this purpose. What then, has happened to its effectiveness?

We suggest here two things: (1) that the church has lost its sense of purpose or has become confused amid the developing complexities of the day; and (2) that it has not understood the purpose of organization and, therefore, how to get into service "able men, such as fear God" who are "full of spirit and wisdom."

If it can be concluded that some organized approach is needed to meet man's spiritual needs, then *organization* must be described in terms others will understand and accept as an integral part of the church. In the doing, we should also explore how we may prepare ourselves to do this.

4

Having had experience in such matters the authors delineate how the application of Christ's teaching together with the application of appropriate management and organization methods succeed in today's church work.

Theme

Throughout the text the author and his co-writer are describing a basic "thought process," or "concept," for operating a church. In their view, this concept for operating a church is the equivalent of a concept for operating a business enterprise which began to evolve in the early thirties. This became known as the "marketing concept." It was eventually defined as a point of view or thinking process which would enable management to successfully operate an entire business in a rapidly changing environment. It originated from the necessity in the early thirties in efforts to pull out of the Great Depression. It took many years to be completely understood and embraced by industry.

Universality of Problems

Because the book deals with a basic thought process, or concept, its advice applies to all denominations of the church—not exclusively to the Baptish church, from which its major case histories are drawn, and which represents the author's own experience. His co-writer, by the circumstances of his life experience, was obliged to move frequently from place to place. In so doing, he adopted the church most convenient to each location. These included originally the Methodist, then Baptist, Congregational, Episcopal, and Presbyterian churches. Exposure to the various denominations was convincing evidence of the universality of problems in the church.

Renewal

The authors recognize and emphasize that actual church renewal can be done only by the Holy Spirit. They know that structural changes and methods in themselves cannot accomplish this. They

do, however, show that dedicated individuals, through corporate planning and methods, provide the channels necessary for the work of the Holy Spirit.

Objective

The objective here is to provide pastors and laymen with a *handbook designed to* show how church activities may be used to cause the growth of individuals, and then in turn to exercise the leadership of others, which in their turn will cause others to want to become part of God's church and its activities. This process is intended to provide the organizational framework with which the church may provide strong spiritual leadership and become again a major influence in the development of human life and a major center of community activities.

I

Planning

Why Planning Is Necessary and What It Is

It does not take much strength to do things, but it requires great strength to decide what to do.

Elbert Hubbard

Background

Our social and economic system is based on the consumption of more and more goods and services to make life "easier and better." People are today caught in a vast communications web in which billions of dollars are spent to persuade them to put a larger and larger share of spendable income into more goods and services. The church competes for people's time, attention, and interest with a comparatively meager piece of this communication machine. Its need for planning of whatever it does, therefore, requires at least as professional a kind of planning as that which goes into the commercial side. It is an axiom in business today that events or activities which are not planned have little chance of occupying even a small corner of the market. Failure of an activity to have a highly developed plan virtually foretells its doom.

Hence, since the church plan must compete with every other conceivable plan, it needs to be made well enough and strategically enough to negate the huge handicap. God's power and help will make up for the difference if the right planning effort is given. But

7

just as the farmer's corn crop cannot be left to God alone, so neither can careful expert planning.

Yet for very many people, plans and planning are very loose concepts. The process of creating a plan—what it takes to come by a really good plan—is poorly understood. For example, few people would consider starting on a journey without having first decided on a destination, a route, and a method of travel, activities to pursue along the way; the cost; and whether it is worth the cost and effort.

A little research reveals that congregations, parishes, and individual church units by the thousands find themselves on a journey whose destination and purpose are not known. More often than not, an aimless drifting or wandering is taking place, and the only change that occurs is an occasional change in "skippers" (pastors). Neither the skipper nor the crew will be happy under these circumstances for long. Either the skipper will abandon ship or the crew will throw him overboard.

But it need not be that way. A course can be charted and a plan developed. The solution lies in the selection of a small but dedicated long-range planning committee that is willing to accept a few simple time-proven planning principles. It should be a small unit with at least one, if possible, who has had some experience with planning principles.

Principles of Planning

Principles of planning for the church may follow those used by industry in business planning for periods of from five to twenty years. These generally recognize at least five basic points:

1. *Analysis* and *statement of the problem*, together with the development of a philosophy around which to build.
2. A set of integrated objectives
3. A set of integrated policies to guide achievement
4. A description of methods or strategies to be applied
5. A description of the kinds of action to be taken—when and by whom.

The development of these five ingredients leads to the establishment of an organization and a selection of people.

The same principles or steps are equally applicable to church planning, but may be called by different names, or may cover the

same points in different ways. But regardless of such variations, the purpose is to

Establish a basic purpose,
Spell out a set of objectives,
Establish priorities and a sequence of events,
Communicate it to the congregation,
Have the entire congregation committed to the common task.

Analysis of Problems

Chance favors the prepared mind

Louis Pasteur

Before we take up the specific details and steps in analyzing the problems of a particular church, we believe that it is imperative that we review the basic problem of the church-at-large and what has happened here in America. With this discussion as a background, it will be easier to identify local problems and gather essential data and other information with which to map out a local plan.

Many have written and preached about the problems of the church today; and with scarcely any exception, they concur that the church is not now fulfilling its mission here in America. It has been observed that America is becoming recognized as the most lawless nation on earth, with about 90 percent of its criminals adolescents. Where do we look for the reasons? Several ugly facts may help.

Today, two-thirds of Protestants do not go to church—their children do not go to a Sunday school. Approximately two out of three Protestant boys and girls in America are not being reached by the Bible study schools. And it is reported that three out of four who enter the Bible study school eventually drop out. On the average, a child entering Sunday school at four receives about 170 hours of religious instruction in a period of about ten years. This compares with approximately 12,000 hours of instruction in secular subjects in the public school system.

Yet jurists particularly—and some statesmen—have declared that what has been called the Sunday school is the antidote to delinquency, and is our best institution for giving boys and girls the God-given fundamentals on which our free democratic institutions

9

were built and upon which it must depend.

In colonial days, 106 of the first 109 colleges were founded by the church. Thus the church recognized that our kind of free society depended on adherence to the Christian discipline, that it had a responsibility not only to evangelize, but to serve other needs of the community. Hence, it took the responsibility for higher education—a function which it allowed the government to take over in later years.

As one commentator puts it, in this century we have seen the passing of the "teaching pastor," the "teaching parent" (not giving elementary religious instruction), the American home with its family altar, and the Bible in our public schools. Yet all of these were basic to our early beginning and national strength.

We certainly need to examine what underlies this state of our affairs. Again, several observations may help.

Many churches tend to reach and preach very largely to their own existing members, making only a minimum effort to reach out to other people in the community who need the help of the church. Further, the emphasis has shifted from spiritual development to predominantly secular and social considerations. This is not intended to imply that the secular and social are unimportant. But without continuing major emphasis on spiritual development of the church's own constituency, individual members rarely live a disciplined Christian life—the major condition for a true leadership role in life.

This falling away of the system for providing spiritual growth and development of the young now poses the greatest challenge of all time for the Protestant church.

Our children and our nation are now the product of what their parents (and perhaps their parents before them) did or did not do about Christian teaching. The children of today will be the church of tomorrow (and the nation).

All this simply means that Bible study must become the *main* business of the church—for children certainly, but for adults as well. It must become the great workshop in which all are engaged.

The reaching of children is the greatest part of what is called evangelism—a term which doubtless very few today really have stopped to consider. But it is not just the evangelism of a Billy Graham. It is the job of the laymen, going into homes, inviting and bringing children and parents into the church school, where they may be taught and shown what Christian caring and love really mean. It has been demonstrated that as a Sunday school grows and prospers, so grows the church. Problems of attendance at the worship service tend to diminish as do the problems of giving and financing. Further, the church school is the means of giving every church member a worthwhile job to do and a chance to participate which feeds on itself.

It is significant to note that the Presbyterian church has recently gone through an agonizing process, lasting several years, to finally recognize and affirm that, with the changing times, its major mission now is here at home and specifically in the local community, where the real problems lie.

Thus, our discussion of the problems of the church-at-large irrevocably brings us to the urgency of re-adopting the Christian philosophy and the function of teaching. It should help us focus on establishing as the main objective and number one priority—the reaching and teaching of the young and the participation of adults as students, teachers, searchers, and visitation specialists.

The National Problem Is a Local Problem

Seeing the problem of the church-at-large in perspective should help greatly in discerning what the problems of a given local church may be. It is often heard that attendance is the problem, or that people will not give enough money to support the church, or that the church is in an old community that no longer has any growth prospects, and so on. Are these the *real* problems? Or are they the symptoms that should be leading to identification of the real causes?

Actually, if people do not attend or will not give money, then the *real* problem is that the message or program simply is not good enough to make people want to come or to give. Development of the spiritual aspect of man is the only thing that the organized church can hope to do better than other institutions. Merely providing a facility for worship or for teaching or for social activities gives insufficient incentive. There must be a program that will search out people who need help, and give it. And today they are the two-thirds mentioned previously who are outside any church, including the children who may be becoming or are already delinquents.

11

With our mobile society, in which one out of five urban and suburban families moves every year, we have at any given moment a high percentage of the community which is transient, which has no roots, and which is very likely to have no sense of belonging anywhere. They should become the business of the church. But the local church may have to overhaul its sense of mission in order to come to grips with its problem.

The lesson here is that to adequately analyze the problem, it is necessary to go very deeply into local conditions, and having identified them, to make sure that the church does not turn its back on those with real needs, who are crying out for help.

There is no amount of so-called planning that will be worth the effort if the analysis is skimpy or if the hard-core problems are not faced, or if the congregation is unwilling to commit itself to doing the necessary. There must be a clear focus and consensus in making the main business of the church the going out to where the problems are and showing how God's plan for living ends frustration, loneliness, and despair. Once this is embraced, planning takes on purpose. This establishes a perspective. Objectives can be stated, guiding policies and methods can be visualized. Every aspect of the church program can be geared to play a supporting role. Further, with the program written down it is capable of being communicated to the congregation and the community.

With this overview of problems of the church at large and how these issue from the local problems, we are now ready to take up the steps of planning for the church.

Planning Steps

Don't wait for something to turn up.
Get a spade and dig for it.

Anonymous

A. Surveys

A study of the environment in which your church operates is paramount to success. So very often, attempts to plan are made without sufficient facts—ending with objectives and steps to

12

solve the wrong problems or nonexistent problems. In industry, no management will give consideration to any planning that has not been based on thorough research. The old seat-of-the-pants approach is gone.

Our study must include development of and carefully cataloged information in at least the following categories:

1. Historical
   (a) Membership—ten years—growth
       By types (baptism, letter, age)
       Attendance by age groups
       Number of families, size, age, years of residence
       Types of professions, trades, education, widowed, retired
       Number in family working
       Income levels
       Geographic areas represented in church membership
   (b) Community composition (normal church radius)
       Population and population growth—twenty years or three census periods
       Present population division (city, county, township, borough)
       By school districts, by schools
       Average family income—growth figures
       Student population by age, grades
       Business climate—principle occupations
       Mobility of families
       Percent of area for development
       Percent of population attending church
   (c) Obtaining information
       It is recognized that obtaining information is a task that will call for considerable effort, and therefore must be assigned to a task force. Although the "first round" of information is the most difficult and time consuming, it should be viewed from the start and planned for as much as possible, as a continuing process, so that the church may have an up-to-date running record of composition and changes. Too often, the organization that succeeded initially is allowed to fall apart—and the church continues to try to operate on old, obsolete information for years afterward.

The information within the church is the first to be assembled and analyzed, and missing information gathered. What the church does not know about itself is generally appalling.

Once the internal job is done, the external information gathering takes on the aspect of an enlightened and objective task—*you know why you need the information.*

(*d*) Sources of outside information:

Religious census of community (described in chapter four)

School board records—plans by age groups

Telephone company—excellent picture of growth

IRS—average family income

Chamber of commerce—basic data on changing aspect of community

Banks—similar to chamber of commerce

Sewer authority—similar to chamber of commerce

Of special importance in analyzing the problem is the establishment of an up-to-date profile of members. Since one of the constant problems in church dynamics is identification of talent for various tasks—leaders, for example— responsibility for this information should be given to a very carefully selected task force.

Should your church not have many of the data needed, then by all means start a record system and you will shortly have enough to greatly improve your efforts. In some instances, a card index system has proved very useful. Presently consideration is being given in one large synod to placing all records on a computer. This latter move will eliminate the aspect of starting all over every time the church officers and personnel change. It is not necessary to own a computer. There are organizations which lease computer time.

B. Calculations and Significance

From the information gathered, other data and "discoveries" can be made.

By comparing church membership with population, it is possible to establish quite accurately what percentage of the popula-

14

tion (and families) the local church has served in the past and to project the size of the congregation for the next five to ten years. The two following charts show how this information was charted to achieve such a projection (a projection which proved to be very accurate).

1961 DATA

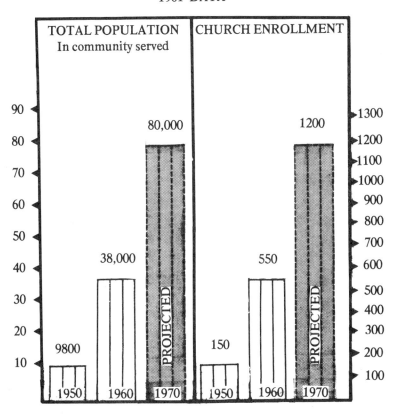

Fig. 1.1. Planning Chart.

15

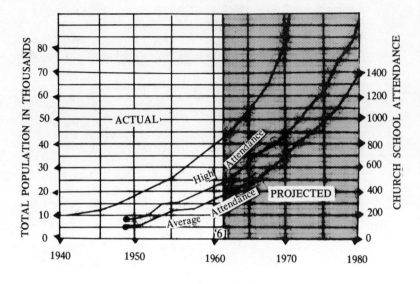

Fig. 1.2. Planning chart.

Data on members, church income, average income per member, and average family income can be tabulated as shown in the following chart to produce estimated annual church income, based on percent of income, for future years. The validity of this approach has become history in several churches.

Should your projection show very small church growth in future years based on its historical percentage of population, it would be well to consider whether or not it should have a more dynamic role in the future. Assuming that it does, then the population must be very closely analyzed. This may be done through a religious census (described in chapter four). Lists may be analyzed by age groups and compared with the church roles to determine which ones are to be called on.

Analysis of this information can then be used to estimate the size and kind of outreach program (including the number of potential teachers and the size of the Bible study school facility) to enlist the young and old who are outside any church.

There are other factors to be studied in relation to how your church is going to be more effective than in the past. What has changed that may cause the future to be different?

Table 1-A

FINANCIAL HISTORY AND PROJECTION

Year	Resident Members	Families	Church Income	Average Income per Member	Estimated Average Family Income (1)	Annual Church Income if Each Family Gave Following Percentage of Income to Church					
							2%	3%	4%	5%	10%
1957	339	—	$ 31,000	$ 91.50							
1958	384	—	36,000	93.80							
1959	416	—	40,000	96.20							
1960	461	—	42,500	92.30							
1961	474	—	45,700	96.50							
1962	512	256	51,600	101.00	$ 6,200	$1,590,000	$ 31,800	$ 47,700	$ 63,600	$ 79,500	$159,000
1963	584	272	59,100	97.00							
1964	642	—	64,900	101.00							
1965	687	278	80,100	116.00							
1966	735 (3)	295	83,000 (2)	120.00 (2)	7,900	2,330,000	46,600	69,900	93,200	116,500	233,000
1967	741	310	94,725	127.00	8,500	2,640,000	52,800	79,200	105,600	132,000	264,000
1968	786	327	106,000								
1969	835	348	120,000								
1970	885	369	135,000	152.00	9,000	3,319,500	66,390	99,580	132,780	165,975	331,950
1971	940	391	149,000								
1972	1,000	416	164,000								
1973	1,075	449	180,000								
1974	1,140	475	197,000								
1975	1,210	505	215,000	177.00	9,750	4,926,500	98,530	147,795	197,060	246,325	492,650
1976	1,290	538	236,000								
1977	1,370	571	260,000	190.00	10,050	5,750,000	115,000	172,500	230,000	287,500	575,000

(1) Based on published Government figures for Bethel Park, South Park Township and Peters Township. Approximately 35% of families have more than one wage earner.

(2) Does not include special gifts such as organ, carillon and donated work associated with construction.

(3) Church roll revised to eliminate those that have moved away or whereabouts unknown for several years.

C. Observations, Assumptions, Objectives

Having assembled, studied and visualized all of the information you have developed, you are now ready to determine its significance. A method for doing this is to summarize under the above three categories. This will provide an orderly picture concerning the future of your church, so that it can be effectively communicated to the membership, whose understanding is essential if the participation and support needed from them is to be gained, and so that proposed objectives can be adopted and become the unifying property of all.

The tabulations shown here make use of some of the foregoing data for illustrative purposes.

1. Observations

    (a) This church is serving a growing community. Census figures show population growth, from 9,800 in 1950 to 38,000 in 1960, and the population projected to grow to 80,000 in another ten years.

    (b) Church enrollment grew from 150 in 1950 to 550 in 1960 and was projected at 1,200 in 1970, based solely on the 80,000 population expected and no improved church programs.

    (c) Church school enrollment paralleled church enrollment but was a little higher. Average attendance is approximately 70 percent of enrollment and 80 percent of high attendance. High attendance is to be used in planning space and staff needs.

    (d) The sharp jump in attendance in 1958 came when additional space was provided in a new building. It subsequently happened again in 1965, although not projected on chart.

    (e) The church family was giving about 3 percent of the family income to the church, showing an increase resulting from tithing promotion.

    (f) Giving exceeded planning projections of income.

    (g) The capacity to finance is much greater than the church is experiencing.

    (h) More buildings and staff will be required for the projected growth to occur.

2. Assumptions
   (a) Assume population will continue to grow as projected.
   (b) Assume that church program will be at least as attractive in the future as it was in the past.
   (c) Assume people have a continued desire and ability to grow.
   (d) Assume the church can finance needed facilities and staff when required in the future.
3. Objectives
   (a) Renew and strengthen the faith of each member in the person of Jesus Christ.
   (b) In the light of the findings, to organize the resources of the church to reach out and find men, women, and children in the community who are unchurched, bring to them the Good News of Jesus Christ, bring them into the church, and teach them Christian living.
   (c) Expand the building facility to accommodate at least an 850-seat auditorium by 1966.
   (d) Expand church school space, as an integral part, to accommodate at least 600.
   (e) Expand the staff so that by 1970 there will be a full-time minister of education and a minister of music.
   (f) Change the constitution and by-laws to provide the opportunity to secure better organization and coordination of the larger program.

Exhibit 1-A shows how such a program was presented to the congregation.

In a downtown or mature situation, the data and assumptions may look quite different. That does not mean, however, that the objectives should be significantly different.

Every great mind is a slumbering power until awakened by keen desire and by definite resolution to do.

Edgar F. Roberts

After facts have been gathered and analyzed and a program is established, it must be sold to the congregation—not en masse, but sold to individuals. One proven way—the same that is used in industry—is to study each prospect and tailor the selling to him. Some will have to be convinced; some are always standing in the wings waiting to be asked. The way to succeed is by knowing everything about each prospect. Many churches depend on an every member canvas to raise money—to get pledges—without really knowing the people they call on or having a well-developed plan to present. Asking for money is difficult enough without encumbering the task through ignorance of the prospect. And prospects can be counted on to resist the usual begging visit. The job should be divided into four parts:

1. Obtaining the profile—finding all about the individuals who make up the congregation
2. Selecting individuals who can make "professional" contributions of talent in evolving an outstanding program
3. Developing a program
4. Organizing a campaign of visits to sell the program to the members and prospective members, *to make them want to be a part of such a program.* Having sold the program, money to support it can be solicited painlessly.

With this done, the annual "every member begging campaign" can be eliminated and squeezed into one great day of giving. With a worthy program effectively communicated and "sold," the monster of money raising evaporates. (See chapter five)

EXHIBIT 1-A

**YOUR
CHURCH
AND ITS
FUTURE**

Presented by

THE PLANNING COMMITTEE
MARCH 1968

A WORD FROM OUR PASTOR...

The following thoughts were presented in the 1962 planning committee report. They seem just as appropriate now as they did then—appropriate because new opportunities are being laid before us and because of your faithful response to previous challenges.

Nehemiah, a man who faced up to the challenges of his hour, led the people to success in restoring the walls of Jerusalem and reestablishing civil authority. This accomplishment was made possible for the following reasons:

1. *He moved in the strength of the Lord.*
   Nehemiah 2:18 (see v. 8) . . . "Told them of the hand of my God which was good upon me." He never could have done what he did in his own strength. Neither can a church build to the glory of God when it looks only at its available means. "Man's extremity becomes God's opportunity."
2. *The People had a mind to work.*
   Nehemiah 2:18b—"So, they strengthened their hands for this good work." They set themselves like a flint to accomplish the task. Everyone had a share in the God-given calling, from the youngest to the oldest, and the poorest to the richest of them. And, in spite of the scorners and the skeptics (Sanballat, Tobiah, and Geshem), they moved tirelessly ahead.
3. *They believed that God would bring the victory.*
   Nehemiah 2:20—"The God of heaven He will prosper us; Therefore we his servants will arise and build." Any enterprise entered into with the sole purpose of glorifying God in the community, and fortified with His Spirit's sanction, cannot fail. Notice that the people put feet to their faith and moved out on the promise—they arose and built! Their labor was crowned with success. Nehemiah 4:6—"So built we the wall."

As members of the church, "an open effectual door has been set before us." May God give us the spiritual vitality to walk through it. To Him be the Glory!

Pastor

"You did well to have it in your heart to build a house for My name."
I Kings 8:18

INTRODUCTION

In 1961-62 the planning committee made comprehensive studies relating to the then current needs of our church and from these studies projected future requirements. Guidelines were recommended to be followed in attaining those needs. While there have been deviations from the original plans, they have provided the direction in which we have grown.

We should be thankful for the foresight of that group for, from this organized planning, we have made unusual progress in all phases of our growth. We should also be thankful for those officers and members who have worked to make the plans a reality.

God has blessed us and rewarded our efforts. A brief review will refresh our memories and serve to inform more recent members of significant accomplishments of the past five years.

1. There have been 195 professions of faith and baptisms.
2. Mission giving increased from $11,661 to $15,860.
3. Church school enrollment increased from 618 to 760.
4. Resident membership increased from 512 to 741.
5. A new 850-seat capacity sanctuary and office space was built.
6. The Philips property was purchased to make room for the new building.
7. The property to the rear of the church was purchased and developed for parking.
8. The total cash income has grown from $59,097 to $94,725.

It is a tribute to the earlier planning committee and the work of all that the 1962 projections of population, membership, attendance, and income have proven remarkably accurate, although generally on the conservative side. Indeed, God has blessed us as we have strived together.

THE FUTURE

The following pages present the results of current studies and projections of needs to give direction to further long-range growth.

Growth

To determine future needs, once again we have looked at population growth in Bethel Park, Peters Township, and South Park Township. Membership and income through 1977 have been projected (see table 1).

Average family incomes as available from the government were used. This same method was used in 1962 and proved conservative for our church.

Buildings

From the growth figures, it appears that the 1962 projections for building needs and priorities are still valid. The master plot plan following has only one building deviation from the original and that is the elimination of a small separate chapel building (see plot plan). Alterations for and/or additional educational space as outlined probably will be required within five years to permit continued orderly growth and effective teaching.

Finances

Our current mortgage balance is $316,598 as of March 1, 1968. Table 1 indicates the income by 1975 should be $215,000. Since previous projections were conservative, this may prove to be likewise.

Recognizing that there will be increased expenses in payroll and maintenance as we grow, and that mission giving should continue to increase, it appears that we can amortize our mortgage faster than required and finance any other requirements as now planned. In other words, we have the ability to finance; our real challenge will be to follow God's leading.

Outside Space Utilization

The master plot plan shows the recommendation for development of the grounds. This provides excellent parking and recreational facilities, covered later.

Recreation

Outside recreation facilities are recommended as shown on the master plot plan. This is the same as the plan presented in conjunction with "Opportunity Sunday" in 1967.

In addition, the old auditorium should be altered as soon as possible so it can be used for the dual purpose of education and indoor recreation. While it is believed that our athletic teams can be a ministry to win people to Christ and enhance Christian growth, we feel it will be more effective if a requirement is made for regular participation in at least one of the following: (1) church worship, (2) Sunday School, (3) training union, (4) choir program. We should continue to participate in church or community league programs of baseball, basketball, or other athletic events when there is sufficient interest among our membership and costs to participate are compatible with our ability to support.

25

Staff Requirements

The following chart shows the full-time staff we should plan to acquire over the next ten years:

Minister of Education	Minister of Counseling
Minister of Music	Hostess
Minister of Youth Work	Additional Custodian
Minister of Children's Work	Additional Secretary

While lay people are filling some of these offices presently, and would continue working in all of them, larger churches that are growing and doing effective work have found it desirable to have professionally trained personnel.

For immediate consideration it is suggested that we add a Minister of Education rather than another Assistant Pastor. A specialist of this type will be more effective and also less likely to seek a church of his own pastorate. The additional specialists listed above should be added one per year as quickly as budgets will permit.

Missions

Two specific objectives are recommended:

1. We should strive toward a minimum of one-third of our budget going to support missionary programs of our denomination in cooperation with our sister churches.
2. We should plan to become the mother church to a mission church in this general area by the time we reach a membership of 1,000. This should be in a community that needs a Baptist witness and one where a small nucleus of our members live who could become the charter members of the new church.

We should keep ever in mind that our commission is to "go into all the world" with the Gospel.

Constitution and Bylaws

More time has been spent on the needs of our church in this area than perhaps any other. The experience of many others has been considered and related to our present and future plans. Some revisions are necessary if the various officers, boards, and committees are to function effectively as a unit. Our present constitution has served us well, but our growth in size and professional ministers requires changes which will provide the necessary coordination and administrative controls. A draft of a revised constitution and bylaws has already been mailed to the membership to be considered at the April 1968 business meeting.

Most changes are relatively minor, as you will note from reading it. These include (1) increasing the number required for a quorum at a Business meeting from 41 to 51, (2) increasing the size of the deacon board, (3) providing for the office of calling outreach, (4) providing for the office of athletic director, (5) composition of a finance committee.

The most significant changes would be the following:

1. Creation of a steering committee to coordinate the work of all boards, committees, etc.
2. Assignment of more specific responsibilities to the elected boards.
3. Support of the elected Sunday School superintendent and training union director by a professionally trained minister of education and the phasing out of the board of education.

The following organizational chart shows the proposed relationships.

ORGANIZATION CHART

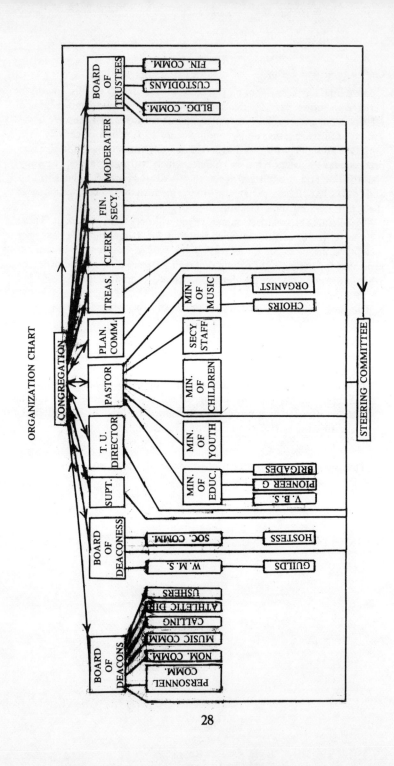

CHRISTIAN RESPONSIBILITY IN THE COMMUNITY

When the mother of two of the apostles came to Jesus with the request that her two sons be granted the privilege of sitting on the right and left hand of Christ, Jesus told her that "the Son of Man came not to be ministered unto but to minister and to give His life a ransom for many." He thus set the pattern for Christian service for all to follow. If Christ Himself came to minister, how much more His followers must recognize that we have a ministering work to do. And also how much more the church as a group of Christians and responsible members of the community, have a service to perform.

How can we as a church minister unto our community? First of all, we have been entrusted with the gospel and it is our responsibility to make it known to all possible. This entails having suitable facilities, where people can come and hear Bible-centered preaching, may come to know the plan of Salvation, may place faith in Him whom to know is Life and Life Eternal, and providing the teaching and the facilities in which the children of all who desire can be taught to know God, to revere and love Him. Secondly, it is the responsibility of helping Christians to grow in the faith, to provide a place for wholesome Christian instruction and fellowship. Thirdly, we have the responsibility of being an example, an example to the community in furthering Christian principles, and taking the initiative to see that a wholesome Christian atmosphere pervades the community. We are also an example to other churches in the community and in the Baptist Association. Thus, we have the opportunity to lead the way in showing how children can be reached with the Gospel through our Sunday School, how unchurched members of our community can be reached by calling and concern for their welfare, and how members of our church can live and work together in harmony, love, and in concern for each other.

Finally, we have the responsibility to alleviate as much suffering as possible in our community, showing a genuine Christian concern for those needing a helping hand.

In these and in other ways, we as a church have a responsibility to our community; and with this service will come the requirement of improved and enlarged facilities. Such service and such facilities will require the self-sacrifice and self-discipline of each member of the church. We believe that our people are ready to move forward for God, under the leadership of the Holy Spirit.

Table 1-A

Year	Resident Members	Resident Families	Church Income	Average Income per Member	Estimated Average Family Income (1)	Annual Church Income if Each Family Gave Following Percentage of Income to Church 2%	3%	4%	5%	10%
1957	339	—	$ 31,000	$ 91.50						
1958	384	—	36,000	93.80						
1959	416	—	40,000	96.20						
1960	461	—	42,500	92.30						
1961	474	—	45,700	96.50						
1962	512	256	51,600	101.00	$ 6,200	$1,590,000	$ 31,800	$ 47,700	$ 63,600	$ 79,500	$159,000
1963	584	272	59,100	97.00						
1964	642	—	64,900	101.00						
1965	687	278	80,100	116.00						
1966	735 (3)	295	83,000 (2)	120.00 (2)	7,900	2,330,000	46,600	69,900	93,200	116,500	233,000
1967	741	310	94,725	127.00	8,500	2,640,000	52,800	79,200	105,600	132,000	264,000
1968	786	327	106,000							
1969	835	348	120,000							
1970	885	369	135,000	152.00	9,000	3,319,500	66,390	99,580	132,780	165,975	331,950
1971	940	391	149,000							
1972	1,000	416	164,000							
1973	1,075	449	180,000							
1974	1,140	475	197,000							
1975	1,210	505	215,000	177.00	9,750	4,926,500	98,530	147,795	197,060	246,325	492,650
1976	1,290	538	236,000							
1977	1,370	571	260,000	190.00	10,050	5,750,000	115,000	172,500	230,000	287,500	575,000

(1) Based on published Government figures for Bethel Park, South Park Township and Peters Township. Approximately 35% of families have more than one wage earner.

(2) Does not include special gifts such as organ, carillon and donated work associated with construction.

(3) Church roll revised to eliminate those that have moved away or whereabouts unknown for several years.

SUMMARY

The planning committee has attempted to outline a comprehensive plan for the church. They have worked prayerfully with a sincere desire to do God's will and help our church grown in Christian faith, carrying God's work to more and more souls all over the world, both at home and abroad. We are hopeful that the membership, officers, boards, and committees will continue to implement the plans in the same energetic way they have in the past and that the praise and glory of the program will be in the name of our Savior, Jesus Christ.

II

Organization

When skill and love work together, expect a masterpiece.

Anonymous

No one method is best for everyone. Two are discussed here to illustrate principles which should help you to decide for your situation. Consider first the most appropriate way to proceed—whether it would be better to evolve into a new structure over a two- or three-year period of time or to make an immediate change. This should be determined by the degree of understanding and support of the plan by the church leaders.

Some churches structure their organization around separate functions, such as education, business, etc., and set up a governing board for each function. The board members are elected by the congregation and report only to the congregation. The major weakness of this approach is the usual lack of coordination of the several functions that make up the whole church. This lack of coordination leads to fragmentation and this, in turn, to disunity. Board members tend to be selected on the basis of their primary interest and seldom are informed as to how their function relates to others organizationally or in importance. More often than not, each person is left to decide, independently or as a particular board, without consultation with other boards.

For instance, in the following type structure,

Approach I

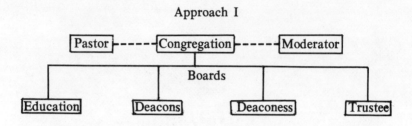

the board of education probably would view its function as being responsible for the complete educational program of the church. Some would act only in regard to the church school, with other training or educational functions scattered elsewhere. In some cases, the church school superintendent is elected directly by the congregation and may only casually relate to the education board, particularly if he is also serving on one of the other boards.

The board of deacons all too often evolves into an image of the "wise men," whose function is to sit back in review of everyone else—to let everyone know when he is off course. Deacons, as in the biblical reference, should be full of wisdom and fear the Lord, but so should the other leadership of the church.

Trustees, on the other hand, usually are in custody of all property, raising of funds, and financing of all other activities. Yet we've seen more than one trustee board whose members tended to be inactive in church affairs and, as a result, had very little firsthand knowledge of the needs of various functions. They perform as though their only understanding of the job were to restrict spending by all in order to comply with income. No effort was made to encourage people to give, let alone tithe.

Deaconesses—well, someone has to prepare the meals for church dinners and help clean up the place once in a while. Oh, yes, and who else will promote missions?

Do not misunderstand—none of the preceding comments are meant to disparage the offices or represent the author's views, but are firsthand observations of what happens in too many churches and reflects a basic weakness. This organizational structure *can* work, but it requires that a comprehensive description of what the people want each board to do be written that every area of activity is assigned to one of the boards, and that some things are not left to chance.

Coordination remains a basic problem with this structure. Some churches have made progress in overcoming this difficulty by superimposing a coordinating council over the boards. The council may be composed of the board chairmen, the pastor, moderator, and any other church officers elected directly by the congregation.

The following one-board principle appears to be a much better approach.

Approach II

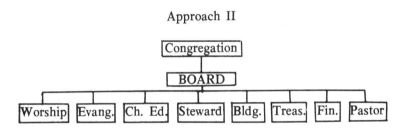

In this approach, each board member is elected to oversee a particular activity, but collectively must hear reports and recommendations and act on the entire church program. Depending on the size of the congregation, each board member may be assigned to carry out one function alone for a very small church, or serve as the chairman of a committee responsible for the function, if the church is large. In this latter case, the balance of the committee should be appointed by the chairman in consultation with the board chairman and the pastor. An example of the functioning of this system follows.

Mr. Snow is elected to fill the Christian education position of the board. As such, Mr. Snow automatically becomes church school superintendent or director. Under the conditions of a small church with a teaching staff of ten or less, Mr. Snow would probably ask each teacher to serve on the Christian education committee. In a larger situation, the department superintendents would probably serve with him to make up the committee.

Under any set of circumstances, it should not be a condition of membership on the committee that everyone be a teacher or worker in the education process of the church. There may well be someone by training, interest, or wisdom of thought, who is well qualified, who could make a significant contribution to the committee, but who has a work schedule or a health condition which prevents the weekly attendance necessary for teaching. This thought should be kept in mind in filling all jobs. Clarity of thought process and spiritual motivation should be significant reasons for considering any person for a church job. Experience alone may be the poorest reason. Some people have had experience—a bad experience repeated a thousand times—which really is worse than none. Each one of us has had to take a job for the first time and learn to do the job correctly. If we are to develop a broad spiritual depth within a congregation, it must include training for and service in functions of the church.

Now you may ask a very valid question or two—how do you discover and enlist people in the organization? Also, how do you make a change if you happen to get someone in the wrong job (a square peg in a round hole)—and you will!

In most churches, you will find people who earn their living in industry, government, or education who are selecting people for specific jobs all the time. They may not think of themselves as "experts," but probably have been successful in their chosen field primarily because they possess leadership qualities and abilities that permit them to learn about, understand, and motivate people. Find and enlist such a person as chairman of a personnel committee (very small) to serve in this capacity. This person is also likely to be persuasive, because he is likely to be well prepared before tackling a job and thus communicate well in the process of talking with people about a specific job.

One extremely important point to remember is that every job should be held for a specific period of time, for example: teachers in church school—one year; board members—three years, with one-third elected each year; etc. Most other jobs should also be of one year's duration. Each job should also have a limit as to how many years of continuous service are permitted. These basic guidelines permit early corrections of any personnel mistakes that may have been made, and they also assure that more people are given the opportunity to serve, thereby creating a more informed and active membership. No person whose talents and abilities are not well demonstrated should be first selected for a job of more than one year's duration.

When talking with someone about a job, *tell the whole truth*. This may seem to be an inappropriate statement in a book about the church. Unfortunately, however, many teachers and other church workers have often heard the phrase "It won't take much of your time." Most jobs *will* take *considerable* time if they are done well. To suggest that they will not is to say immediately to the prospect, "We've got low standards around here, so not much is expected."

If we are to help God to make the church of Jesus Christ the influence for good in the world that it was meant to be, we must quit apologizing when we ask a person to serve, and emphasize that it will require considerable time and talent. Since the church is extremely important in the world, and most people want to be involved in important matters, we must start taking every opportunity to demonstrate and visualize. It is vital to show and explain to the prospect specifically what is expected in the job performance, and why you believe that person is the one for the job. Have you ever heard "We can't get anyone else"? Also, explain that if it does not work out, you promise to discuss it with him and make a change. Long service as a church school superintendent verifies this approach and shows that people respect it, and that changes can be made without offending. Consider this example. In talking with Mr. Smith about teaching a class of ninth graders, you would explain the objectives of the church school, characteristics of ninth graders, specific individuals in the class and their needs, why you believe God can use the particular talents of Mr. Smith, information about the literature and how to use it with the basic text of the Bible. You would also explain the various learning opportunities for teachers and other resources. You would explain, by example, how someone else like himself had grown by taking a similar job and some examples of students whose lives had been changed. You would also explain that you would be observing his performance without looking over his shoulder, and be making suggestions from time to time as well as learning from him, in order to share his strengths with other teachers.

When a good job is done in selection, training, and helping, it is not often that a change will need to be made. When those occasions for change do arise, first make sure that all has been done that can be done to help; but then face the issue, by reminding the person of your conversation at the time of selection. Also, make sure you have selected another job, if at all possible, that the person is more suited to do. This may consist of teaching another age group, or it may be something totally different. Because some dedicated, but not very talented, people sincerely want to be of service, there have been occasions when a new job was created to meet a particular individual's needs. God can use all of us. If a high sounding job with minimum requirements is what it takes to meet this person's needs, then create it, make the moves, and get on with the important business at hand.

Another important principle in church organization is the utilization of everyone in some kind of job. This means maintaining small organizational units in areas such as church school classes. This creates more teaching jobs, class presidents, etc. People involved become more interested, and grow and mature as Christians. In addition, small units create a better learning environment. (Children 10-15 enroll; youths 15-20 enroll; adults 25-30 enroll.) It is much less likely for a teacher to inadvertently develop a personal following, which ultimately clogs up the whole system and creates divisiveness. How many times have you seen an adult class become "Uncle Ned's" or "Aunt Samantha's" class? Teachers, pastors, and all workers are *servants*. God is to be glorified. Certainly teachers and all workers are to be honored, but be careful that it does not reach the point where the teacher stands between the student and God, and the student primarily sees the teacher instead of God, and becomes a follower of the teacher.

It is helpful to keep reminding teachers (when the superintendent) or students (when the teacher), that the whole purpose of Bible study is the development of a sensitivity to God, so that when *He* speaks, whether through the teacher, the pastor, and their fellow students, or through Bible reading, worship, and prayer, each will recognize God and follow *His* leadership.

Sensitivity

At this point it seems appropriate to elaborate on sensitivity.

We must be prepared to listen—to hear—and to understand when God is speaking to us as creatures of His creation. Without this sensitivity, we cannot know and understand what we are to do with respect to others—or to follow where He leads us. To illustrate how this sensitivity works, you might consider this demonstration. Scratch your hand. One scratch discolors and then disappears. If you continue, however, the skin wears away and you have a very sensitive spot. In the same way in order to develop a sensitivity to God, we must continue a sensitizing process. Bible study and prayers are the most useful methods.

Approach III

A third method for organizing a church is found in the report of Joseph L. Baker, called "Strategy for Mission Through Small Groups." While it is not possible to give details here, the Summary and Conclusions from this remarkable success story are given in Exhibit 2-A. This is the basis used for the founding of a new church in Fort Wayne, Indiana.

Cassette tapes are available for a nominal sum covering the details of this approach.

Contact: Rev. Joseph L. Baker
Faith Baptist Church
6600 Trier Road
Fort Wayne, Indiana 46805

EXHIBIT 2-A

STRATEGY FOR MISSION
THROUGH SMALL GROUPS

Excerpted from a report
by Joseph L. Baker, 1969

Summary and Conclusions

Summary

This study is the result of the writer's desire to share with others the experiences which have come from the use of small groups in founding the Faith Baptist Church in suburban northeast Fort Wayne, Indiana. This writing is not a critical or an exhaustive study of the effective use of small groups within the church, but more of a report. This report shows that positive results are possible when small groups have been an integral part of the strategy for starting a new church. The material that was surveyed infers that small groups can also become agents of renewal in the established church.

Chapter I presents a detailed account of the birth of an American Baptist church in northeast Fort Wayne, Indiana, that was born through an extensive program of calling and the establishment of small groups. During eighteen months of history, four types of small groups were used for the development of the church. They were called: (1) Study and Planning Groups, (2) Percentage Giving Groups, (3) Adult Inquiry Groups, and (4) Capital Funds Campaign Groups. The data used in this chapter show that the addition of groups is the most basic factor in answering the question, "How does a church grow?"

Chapter II is concerned with personal and church renewal through small groups. The writer shows that broken relationships—man with God and man with man—make spiritual renewal an absolute necessity for man. It is pointed out that reconciliation can best be achieved through the dialogical process of small groups. This chapter defines (1) the objectives of small groups, (2) the structure of small groups, and (3) the program of small groups.

Chapter III presents a biblical base to support the contention that the church is called to be an agent of reconciliation and to become an extension of its Lord's servant ministry in the world. It has been found that small task force groups can be used for Christian ministry within the church and without. Several suggestions are offered to show the kind of action groups needed in many of our churches and communities.

Conclusions

1. The strategy which will best serve the church in mission today consists of formulating and implementing structures that will best achieve the goals of the local church. Whether we are establishing a new church or attempting to renew an established one, it is vitally important that the congregation becomes involved first in determining and then in achieving its own goals.

2. The success story of Faith Baptist Church demonstrates that if goals, or objectives, really grasp us, then our lives can be motivated to achieve relentlessly those desirable ends.

3. We must concede that structural changes within the church will not, in and of themselves, bring about the achievement of desirable goals without the working of the Holy Spirit. We should, however, do what we can in our churches to provide channels through which the Holy Spirit can work. The evidence suggests that one such channel is the effective use of small groups within the church.

4. Evidence supports the conclusion that extensive calling is necessary for establishing a new congregation.

5. Small group experiences proved to be an important catalyst for bringing renewal to fifty previously inactive church families, who became members of the Faith Baptist Church. After eighteen months, forty-five of the fifty families are quite active in the life and mission of the church.

6. Most participants in group study voiced their hopes that Faith Baptist Church would not become a "big" church. It was felt that the chief strength of a small church is the intimate fellowship. The experience through small groups suggest that it is possible for people to develop real and meaningful relationships that equal those in a small church.

7. Evidence proves that successful financial campaigns can be achieved through small groups.

8. Experience shows that four to six couples in a group make for good discussion, yet the group is not too large for meeting in the homes of the participants.

9. The Adult Inquiry Groups provided opportunities for men and women to come to grips with the basic beliefs of Christianity, and to face honestly their doubts and uncertainties. They were not expected to subscribe to tenets which forced them to compromise their integrity, but encouraged them to strive continually to grow in spiritual sensitivity and perceptiveness, all the while laying the groundwork for new experiences in Christian growth and witness. In short, the groups proved to be at their best when there was

an unquenchable thirst for truth—wherever it was found.

10. As a result of hundreds of calls and many hours spent in discussion groups, the writer finds that he is beginning to really listen to persons with different views. He has found that true dialogue takes place when there is a genuine openness and free exchange of ideas between two or more persons. It has been discovered again and again that no one has all the truth. Each one has a part, maybe an important part, but only a part.

11. Evidence shows that a church grows through the addition of new groups.

12. The most effective group is the one which does not exist by and for itself; its true life is to be found *in the church*.

13. It has been found that commitment is a necessary beginning for each member of a small group, but it is far from being the end. Beyond commitment is toil, which cannot be accomplished without the glad acceptance of personal discipline.

14. It should be kept in mind that what we seek in the small group is not a fellowship of the righteous or of the self-righteous, but rather a fellowship of men and women who, recognizing that they are inadequate, nevertheless can become personally involved in the effort of advancing the Kingdom of God in their community.

15. Evidence supports the conclusion that small groups can take many different forms, such as:

a. Reflection-action groups
b. Faith-action groups
c. Prayer and study groups
d. Vocational groupings
e. Lunch or breakfast groups
f. Talk-back groups
g. Parishioner's part in preaching groups
h. Parents without partners groups
i. Koinonia groups
j. Exposure groups

16. Small groups can be a vehicle through which persons can deepen their Christian faith and life. In the final analysis, our churches will be only as strong in relation to the members' ability to "give a reason for the faith that is in them."

17. Small groups can become the channels through which man is reconciled with God and man is reconciled with man.

18. The purpose and nature of small groups can be summed up in the

New Testament admonition to "grow in the grace and knowledge of our Lord and Saviour Jesus Christ" (2 Peter 3:18).

19. Evidence supports the conclusion that the church can minister in the world through task force groups.

III

Constitution and Bylaws

No man is good enough to govern another man without that other's consent.

Abraham Lincoln

A dictionary definition of a constitution is as follows: "The system of fundamental laws and principles that prescribes the nature, functions, and limits of a government or other institution." A bylaw is defined as (1) a secondary law; (2) a law or rule governing the internal affairs of an organization. Many organizations create unnecessary difficulties for themselves by getting into their constitution things that really belong in bylaws. Bylaws should be easy to change. Recognizing that we live in a world of change, and none are sufficiently wise to foresee accurately the future, we should not make it difficult for our successors in the church to change the rules governing the internal affairs. On the other hand, it should be much more difficult (requiring a high percentage of membership in favor) to change the basic principles prescribing the nature of the institution.

In Exhibit 3-A, Articles I and II primarily cover basic principles prescribing the nature of the institution. The exception is the name. Article III, on the other hand, deals primarily with rules governing the internal affairs, although some basic principles are mixed in and should be extracted. Qualifications in principle to be pastor, terms and rotations of office holders, quorum, voting majority required for decision making, and basis for constitutional change are basic principles also. In some things it should not be possible to make changes at all. Two are in Exhibit 3-A, for instance—purpose and character. The purpose is clearly to be a Christian institution, yet there is sufficient latitude to permit diversity in emphasis from evangelism to service. In the character, note the (1) affiliation with American Baptist, (2) government vested in membership, and (3) New Testament acceptance in doctrine and practice. There are all kinds of institutions started by other individuals or groups that will differ on these points; therefore, no individual is being deprived of supporting his own belief by not changing these within an individual church. The free choice to change is from one institution to another with a character more to the liking of the one desiring a change.

Exhibits 3-B and 3-C are additional examples which, along with the principles discussed here, should adequately assist anyone writing or changing the constitution and bylaws of his church.

Exhibit 3-D is an example of a constitution and bylaws of an association of churches.

The combination of organization and constitution and bylaws when properly planned to accommodate the purpose and objectives of a church, and when properly communicated, should easily result in the majority consenting to being governed by the principles set forth. With the brief principles set out above and the examples that follow, it is hoped the reader will be helped in some way.

EXHIBIT 3-A

CONSTITUTION
of the

Revised and Amended November 25, 1974

ARTICLE I

Name

The name of this organization shall be the

Purpose

The purpose of this church shall be to maintain the public worship of God; to seek to bring people to the personal acceptance and confession of the Lord Jesus Christ as Savior and Lord; to provide religious education for both young and old; to help proclaim the Gospel in all the world; to build a Christian brotherhood and join our forces in Christian service.

Character

Section 1. The government of this church is vested in the body which comprises its membership, but because its parish is world-wide, it recognizes its obligation and privilege to cooperate with other religious bodies having the same general objectives. It shall therefore be affiliated with the

Section 2. The church accepts the New Testament as an all-sufficient basis of doctrine and practice. As a summary of principles for Christian conduct among its members, it adopts the church covenant (Appendix A).

ARTICLE II

Membership

Section 1. The membership shall consist of the following:

A. Persons confessing Jesus Christ as their personal Savior and Lord, promising to live the Christian life, and being baptized by immersion.
B. Persons baptized by immersion and presenting letters of recommendation from other Baptist churches.
C. Persons baptized by immersion and coming upon their statement of Christian experience from some other Christian church.

D. Persons not baptized by immersion and coming upon a statement of Christian experience from some other Christian church, who shall be known as associate members.

Section 2. Members shall be received in the following manner:

A. Persons coming upon profession of faith or a statement of Christian experience and desiring baptism shall be interviewed by the board of deacons. Upon the recommendation of the board, such persons shall be received into the membership after baptism.

B. Persons coming by letter from some other Baptist or Christian church shall be interviewed by the board of deacons and upon their recommendation shall be received into the membership.

C. Persons coming as associate members shall be interviewed by the board of deacons and upon their recommendation shall be received into the membership. Associate members shall be entitled to all rights and privileges of the church, except that they shall not be permitted to vote on questions of church polity. (Polity pertains to the constitution of the church.)

D. All persons desiring membership shall be voted upon at a public meeting of the church.

Section 3. Members may be dismissed as follows:

A. By letter. Any member in good and regular standing who desires a letter of dismission and recommendation to any other church is entitled to receive it upon request. The name of the church to which membership is to be transferred must be indicated in the request, and the letter shall be sent to the pastor or clerk of the church. This letter shall be valid as a recommendation for six months from its date, unless renewed, and this restriction shall be stated in the letter.

B. By action of the church. At the recommendation of the board of deacons, when there has been willful neglect of attendance at the services of the church and a lack of interest evidenced by nonsupport of the work of the church, such persons shall be contacted, if possible, and notified of the intention of the church to remove their names from the roll.

ARTICLE III

Officers, Boards and Committees

Pastor

The pastor shall be a regularly ordained minister of the Gospel in the Baptist denomination who shall be a believer in and a preacher of the essential doctrines of faiths as interpreted in the historic life of the Regular Baptist denomination. He shall be called by a three-fourths vote of all the members present and voting at a meeting called for the purpose, provided that two weeks' notice has been publicly given of the meeting. His salary shall be fixed at the time of election, and may be changed at any regular business meeting of the church, upon recommendation of the board of trustees. He shall be elected for no specified term, but three months' notice shall be given by either party of intention to dissolve the relationship.

The pastor shall be an ex officio member of all boards and committees.

Assistant Pastor

Upon recommendation of the board of deacons, an assistant pastor may be called by a three-fourths vote of all the members present voting at a meeting called for the purpose, provided that two weeks' notice has been publicly given of the meeting. His salary shall be fixed at the time of election, and may be changed at any regular business meeting of the church, at the recommendation of the board of trustees. He shall be elected for no specified term, but two months' notice shall be given by either party of intention to dissolve the relationship. He shall be an ex officio member of the board of deacons and the board of Christian education.

Clerk

A church clerk shall be elected at the annual meeting of the church to serve for one year. It shall be the duty of the clerk to keep a record of all business of the church; to keep a correct roll of membership; to issue letters of dismissal to members when granted by the church; to present a written report at the annual church meetings; to prepare the church letter and reports and forward the same to the clerk of the Pittsburgh Baptist Association when it has been approved by the church. All books, records, and papers used by the clerk shall be the property of the church, shall be kept in a safe place, and shall be turned over to a successor in office.

Financial Secretary

A financial secretary shall be elected at the annual meeting of the church to serve for one year. It shall be the duty of the financial secretary to receive all monies of the church, to make a record of the same and then turn over the cash or bank deposit slips to the treasurer of the church. The financial secretary shall give a report at all regular business meetings of the church. An annual report shall be made to the church at the annual meeting.

Treasurer

A treasurer shall be elected at the annual meeting of the church to serve for one year. It shall be the duty of the treasurer to receive from the financial secretary all funds given the church. The treasurer shall make a record of receipts from all sources, and all expenditures, and shall pay all bills authorized by the trustees, appropriate board or organization, or church body. All monies shall be disbursed on the basis of the items with the church approved unified budget. The monthly rate of the unified missionary budget of the denomination shall be forwarded to the state collecting agency at least once a month, to reach the state offices before the fifteenth of the following month. Reports shall be made to the trustees once a month, at all regular business meetings of the church, and at the annual meeting. An appropriate accounting system shall be used that records and reports all expenses in accordance with items in the unified budget.

Board of Deacons

The board of deacons shall consist of at least nine members, elected for terms of three years each; and their terms shall be so arranged that at least three may be elected each year. They shall not be eligible to serve for more than one term of three years without the intervention of one year.

The deacons shall be "men of honest report, full of the Holy Ghost and wisdom." Their duties shall be:

A. To assist the pastor in promoting the spiritual welfare of the church, in the conduct and scheduling of the religious services and in the administration of the ordinances.

B. To review all applications for membership before they are presented to the church body for a vote.

C. To visit the sick and distressed members of the church and, when necessary, relieve their needs by appropriation from the fellowship fund.

Board of Deaconesses

The board of deaconesses shall consist of at least nine members, elected for terms of three years each, and their terms so arranged that at least three may be elected each year. They shall not be eligible for more than one term of three years without the intervention of one year.

The deaconesses shall cooperate with the board of deacons and the pastor in seeking to promote the spiritual welfare of the church, in the care of the poor, the visitation of the sick, the welcoming of new members and the preparation of the communion table.

Board of Trustees

There shall be a Board of at least nine trustees in addition to the church treasurer, who is an ex officio member of the board. At least three trustees shall be elected each year. Their term of office shall be for three years. They shall not be eligible to serve for more than one term of three years without the intervention of one year.

The trustees shall hold in trust all property of the church and shall be responsible for the management of the same. They shall be empowered to hire all employees except the pastor and assistant pastor. They shall not sell or encumber the real estate or other property of the church unless authorized to do so by a three-fourths vote of the members present at a meeting called for the purpose of considering such a transaction. Such a meeting of the church must be called in accordance with the provisions of the laws of the Commonwealth of Pennsylvania, which governs the selling or encumbering of church property.

The trustees shall have responsibility for the maintenance and replacement of church property as needed. They shall not enter into contracts for work or replacement or purchase of new equipment involving a greater sum than $1,000, without the express consent of the church at a regular meeting or a special meeting called for this purpose.

The trustees shall establish a finance committee which shall submit to the church membership in printed form a month before the annual meeting an itemized unified budget of the church expenses for the ensuing year, and shall also be charged with the raising of funds to meet this budget. The finance committee shall be composed of at least three trustees, one deacon, one deaconess, one Christian education board member, one woman's mission society representative, and one representative member of the youth of the church. Each representative shall be responsible for obtaining views on the proposed budget from the organization represented.

Board of Christian Education

The board of Christian education shall consist of at least six elected members, two or more to be elected each year for a term of three years. They shall not be eligible to serve for more than one term of three years without the intervention of one year. The Sunday school superintendent shall be an ex officio member of this board.

This board shall be responsible for the planning and administration of the total educational program of the church school.

This board shall be responsible for turning over to the financial secretary all monies received through the Sunday school. Also, all expenditures against the Sunday school portion of the unified budget shall be approved by this board.

Moderator

A moderator shall be elected from the membership of the church who

48

shall preside at all the business meetings of the church.

The moderator shall be elected in the same way as other officers of the church at the regular church election and shall hold office for one year.

The moderator, in cooperation with the pastor, shall be responsible for the appointment of any church committee not specifically designated in the constitution and bylaws as being appointed or elected otherwise.

Superintendent of the Sunday School

A superintendent of the church school shall be elected at each annual meeting to serve for one year. He shall have general supervision of the church school and present a quarterly report on the program and work of the church school to the church.

Music Committee

The musical ministry of the church shall be supervised by a music committee composed of eight members: one appointed from the board of deacons for a term of one year, one appointed from the board of deaconesses for a term of one year, and six to be elected for terms of three years each, with their terms so arranged that two may be elected each year. The selection of the church organist or any paid musician, and the selection of a choir director shall be the responsibility of this committee. Any expenditure of money, however, shall have the approval of the board of trustees and shall be made through the treasurer of the church.

Auditing Committee

An auditing committee of three members shall be elected at the annual meeting of the church, to serve for one year. It shall be the duty of the auditing committee to make a full examination of the books, accounts, and bills of the church and to make a written statement to the church at the end of the church year or at the close of the term of office of the church treasurer, financial secretary, or any subsequently elected church officer handling church funds.

Nominating Committee

The nominating committee shall consist of five members, one appointed from and by each of the four boards of the church and one by the pastor. The appointees shall be presented to the church and by the moderator or pastor for approval at the first quarterly meeting. They shall serve for one year. This committee shall present one or more nominations for the various offices that become vacant at the expiration of the church year. Those nominated shall be interviewed to secure their consent to accept the office for which nomination is made. Nominations made by this committee shall not be understood to prevent nominations being made from the floor for any office at the annual meeting for election of officers. Should a vacancy occur in any office for any reason during the church year, this committee shall present in nomination a name or names to fill such vacancy at either a regular meeting of the church or a special meeting called for that purpose, provided notice of such special election has been made at least one week previous.

Planning Committee

There shall be a planning committee constituted as follows: the moderator, church clerk, treasurer, financial secretary, superintendent of Sunday school, two members of the board of Christian education, two members of the deacon board, two members of the trustee board, two members of the deaconess board, and four members at large appointed by the pastor, at least two of which shall be members of the young people's department.

The planning committee shall meet prior to the annual meeting of the church or at the call of the pastor. Their responsibility is purely advisory and they shall consider plans for the welfare of the church.

Building Committee

The building committee shall consist of at least nine members, three of whom are to be elected each year at the annual meeting for terms of three years each. It shall be the duty of the committee to properly care for building funds included in the unified budget to be used for the future building program of the church. When authorized to do so by the congregation, they shall plan and supervise new building construction. They shall be governed by the same financial limitations as are imposed upon the board of trustees.

Pulpit Committee

The pulpit committee shall consist of the chairmen of the four boards of the church, the church clerk, the moderator, the Sunday School superintendent, the president of the senior young people's society, and one member appointed by the president of the woman's mission society.

When the pulpit becomes vacant, it shall be the duty of the committee to promptly seek out an accredited minister and present his name to the church for action. Only one name may be presented to the church at a time. The purpose of this provision is that prospective pastors are not put in contest with each other.

Committee on World Mission Support

The committee on world mission support shall consist of six elected members, two members to be elected each year for a term of three years. They shall not be eligible for more than one term of three years without the intervention of one year. The chairman of missionary and stewardship education of the church board of Christian education, and the chairman of the committee on missions of the board of deacons shall serve as ex officio members. It shall be the responsibility of the committee to stimulate and to increase the missionary interest and giving of the church members. Annually it shall recommend to the finance committee the amounts to be included in the church's unified budget for the American Baptist Mission budget. During the year it shall keep the church members informed of their contributions to the denomination's mission budget.

Amendments

This constitution or bylaws may be changed or amended by a three-fourths majority of at least seventy-five members present and voting at any regular or specially called meeting of the church, providing written notice of such change has been given the congregation at least two weeks previous.

BYLAWS

1. There shall be a quarterly business meeting for the transaction of any business that may be necessary and for the receiving of quarterly reports. Such meeting shall be held the second Wednesday evening of each quarter.

2. The annual business meeting of the church shall be held the second Wednesday evening in January, at 8 o'clock, except for the election of church officers. An annual meeting shall be held at 8:00 P.M. on the last Wednesday of November for the purpose of receiving the report of the nominating committee and election of officers for the ensuing year to take office January first.

3. The church shall hold a monthly communion service and such special occasions as approved by the pastor and board of deacons.

4. Upon the written request of the board of deacons or fifteen members of the church, a business meeting must be called, providing the notice and purpose of such a meeting has been placed in the hands of the moderator or church clerk so as to allow for the public announcement of such meeting to be given one week in advance.

5. The pastor shall be granted one month's vacation with full pay each year. The assistant pastor shall be granted one month's vacation with full pay each year, not to run concurrently with the pastor's vacation. The periods of vacation are to be agreed upon by the pastor, assistant pastor, and the deacon board.

6. Delegates to any association or convention may be chosen at any

regular meeting of the church by direct choice of the church or by authorizing the pastor to appoint such delegates.

7. Members to the permanent council of the Baptist Association shall be nominated by the nominating committee and elected at the annual meeting.

8. All questions shall be decided by majority vote, except that of calling a pastor, an assistant pastor, or spending certain amounts of money aforementioned, which require a three-fourths majority. Voting, when so requested, may be by ballot. All voting for official positions in the church or church school shall be by ballot.

9. If a man shall have proved himself a spiritual leader, although no longer capable of assuming the full duties of active leadership, the deacons may nominate him as an honorary deacon for life, and the congregation may elect him as such. An honorary deacon may not vote nor be required to attend regular meetings of the board, but his advice may be sought from time to time.

10. The head usher shall be appointed by the deacons. He shall select and direct the ushers for all regular church services.

11. No member of the board of deacons, deaconesses, trustees, or Christian education may serve on more than one board at the same time.

12. Business meetings shall be conducted in parliamentary procedure in accord with *Robert's Rules of Order.*

13. Quorum: Forty-one members shall constitute a quorum for the transaction of business, including annual budget approval, except when it involves the sale or purchase of property, expenditures not included in approved budget in excess of $1,000, the calling or dismissal of a pastor or assistant pastor, or changes or amendments to the constitution or bylaws. Such transactions shall be valid only when at least seventy-five members are present and a three-fourths majority of the votes cast shall be necessary to validate such action.

14. Fellowship fund: There shall be maintained for the relief of any person in the community, or for such other purposes as approved by the church upon recommendation of the board of deacons, a special fund, which shall be designated as the fellowship fund. This fund shall be maintained as a budget item included in the unified budget and shall be under the control of the board of deacons.

15. The fiscal year of the church shall close December 31 of each calendar year.

16. In the absence of the moderator at any business meeting of the church, it shall be the responsibility of the pastor of the church to preside at such meeting, or to appoint an acting moderator. In the event of the absence of both the moderator and the pastor at a called business meeting, the members present shall appoint a moderator from their own group.

APPENDIX A

The Church Covenant

Having been led, as we believe, by the Spirit of God to receive the Lord Jesus Christ as our savior, and on the profession of our faith, having been baptized in the name of the Father, and of the Son, and of the Holy Ghost, we do now, in the presence of God and angels, most solemnly and joyfully enter into covenant with one another, as one body in Christ.

We engage, therefore, by the aid of the Holy Spirit, to walk together in Christian love:

To strive for the advancement of this church in knowledge, holiness and comfort;

To promote its prosperity and spirituality.

To sustain its worship, ordinances, discipline, and doctrines;

To give it a sacred pre-eminence over all institutions of human origin;

To contribute cheerfully and regularly to the support of the ministry, the expenses of the church, and the relief of the poor, and the spread of the Gospel through all nations.

We also engage to maintain family and secret devotion;

To religiously educate our children;

To seek the salvation of our kindred and acquaintances;

To walk circumspectly in the world;

To be just in our dealings, faithful in our engagements, and exemplary in our deportment;

To avoid all tattling, backbiting, and excessive anger;

To abstain from the sale and use of intoxicating drinks as a beverage, and to be zealous in our efforts to advance the Kingdom of our Savior.

We further engage to watch over one another in brotherly love;

To remember each other in prayer;

To aid each other in sickness and distress;

To cultivate Christian sympathy in feeling and courtesy in speech;

To be slow to take offense, but always ready for reconciliation and mindful of the rules of our Savior, to secure it without delay.

We moreover engage that when we remove from this place, we will as soon as possible unite with some other church, where we can carry out the spirit of this covenant and the principles of God's work.

SUGGESTED CONSTITUTION AND BYLAW CHANGES

Suggested change of reading, under designated headings, as shown on the following pages.

Treasurer

A treasurer shall be elected at the annual meeting of the church to serve for one year. It shall be the duty of the treasurer to receive from the Financial Secretary all funds given the church. The treasurer shall make a record of receipts from all sources, and all expenditures, and shall pay all bills authorized by the trustees, appropriate board of organization, or church body. All monies shall be disbursed on the basis of the items within the church-approved unified budget. The monthly rate of the unified missionary budget of the denomination shall be forwarded to the state collecting agency at least once a month, to reach the state offices before the fifteenth of the following month. Reports shall be made to the trustees once a month, at all regular business meetings of the church, and at the annual meeting. An appropriate accounting system shall be used that records and reports all expenses in accordance with items in the unified budget.

Board of Trustees

(Change the reading of the last paragraph only under this heading, with the remainder of the wording intact)

... The trustees shall establish a finance committee which shall submit to the church membership in printed form, a month before the annual meeting, an itemized unified budget of the church expenses for the ensuing year, and shall also be charged with the raising of funds to meet this budget. The finance committee shall be composed of at least three trustees, one deacon, one deaconess, one Christian education board member, one woman's mission society representative, and one representative member of the youth of the church. Each representative shall be responsible for obtaining views on the proposed budget from the organization represented.

Board of Christian Education

(Change the reading of item b. only to the following.)

b. This board shall be responsible for turning over to the financial secretary all monies received through the Sunday school. Also, all expenditures against the Sunday school portion of the unified budget shall be approved by this board.

Moderator

(Add the following paragraph to the present wording under this heading.)

The moderator in cooperation with the pastor shall be responsible for the appointment of any church committee not specifically designated in the constitution and bylaws as being appointed or elected otherwise.

Auditing Committee

An auditing committee of three members shall be elected at the annual meeting of the church to serve for one year. It shall be the duty of the auditing committee to make a full examination of the books, accounts, and bills of the church and to make a written statement to the church at the end of the church year or at the close of the term of office of the church treasurer, financial secretary, or any subsequently elected church officer handling church funds.

Nominating Committee

The nominating committee shall consist of five members, one appointed from and by each of the four boards of the church and one by the pastor. The appointees shall be presented to the church by the moderator or pastor for approval at the third quarterly meeting. They shall serve for one year. This committee shall present one or more nominations for the various offices that become vacant at the expiration of the church year. Those nominated shall be interviewed to secure their consent to accept the office for which nomination is made. Nominations made by this committee shall not be understood to prevent nominations being made from the floor for any office at the annual meeting for election of officers. Should a vacancy occur in any office for any reason during the church year, this committee shall present in nomination a name or names to fill such vacancy at either a regular meeting of the church, or at a special meeting called for that purpose, provided notice of such special election has been made at least one week previous.

Building Committee

The Building committee shall consist of at least nine members, three of whom are to be elected each year at the annual meeting for terms of three years each. It shall be the duty of the committee to properly care for building funds included in the unified budget to be used for the future building program of the church. When authorized to do so by the congregation, they shall plan and supervise new building construction. They shall be governed by the same financial limitations as are imposed upon the board of trustees.

Bylaws

1. Quarterly meetings shall be held the second Wednesday of each quarter.

2. The annual business meeting of the church shall be held the second Wednesday evening in January, at 8:00 P.M., except for the election of church officers. An annual meeting shall be held at 8:00 P.M. on the last

Wednesday of November for the purpose of receiving the report of the Nominating Committee and election of officers for the ensuing year to take office January first.

13. Quorum: Forty-one members shall constitute a quorum for the transaction of business, including annual budget approval, except when it involves the sale or purchase of property, expenditures not included in approved budget in excess of $1,000 the calling or dismissal of a pastor or assistant pastor, or changes or amendments to the constitution or bylaws. Such transactions shall be valid only when at least seventy-five members and a three-fourths majority of the votes cast shall be necessary to validate such action.

14. Fellowship fund: There shall be maintained for the relief of any person in the community, or for such other purposes as approved by the church upon recommendation of the board of deacons, a special fund which shall be designated as the fellowship fund. This fund shall be maintained as a budget item included in the unified budget and shall be under the control of the board of deacons.

EXHIBIT 3-B

CONSTITUTION

ARTICLE I—NAME

The name of this church shall be   , also referred to in this constitution as "the Fellowship."

ARTICLE II—AFFILIATION

The church shall maintain affiliation and cooperation with

ARTICLE III—PURPOSE

The purpose of this church shall be (1) to persuade and assist people in adopting *The Way* of living which is under the control and possession of God; (2) with Jesus Christ as head and the Bible as authority, to become a fellowship which embodies *The Way*; (3) with the Holy Spirit as strategist and leader, to launch or engage in whatever mission of service to mankind He may direct in the name of Jesus; and (4) to encourage and equip members of *The Way* as individuals to carry its principles out into the conduct of the world's business in which they are engaged.

ARTICLE IV—MEMBERSHIP

Section A—Qualifications. Membership in this church shall be open to anyone having reached the age of discretion who

1. desires to be under the control and possession of God;
2. accepts Jesus Christ as head and the Bible as authority;
3. is willing to be a regular and responsible part of the Fellowship including
   a. weekly worship and study with the Fellowship,
   b. some form of service in the Fellowship or through one of its mission projects,
   c. systematic and recorded giving of funds toward underwriting the budget of the church;
4. agrees to abide by this constitution and any bylaws the church may, enact under Article XII hereof.

Section B—Joining the Church. Upon a candidate's public assent to each of the qualifications above, made before the congregation at any meeting thereof, he shall be given the "Right Hand of Fellowship," officially marking his membership in the church. (No other examination of the candidate, and no vote of the congregation shall be required.) A candidate may join in any of the following ways:

1. *Baptism,* which shall be administered by immersion to believers only;
2. *Letter of transfer* from any Christian church;
3. *Profession of faith* in cases where records of previous church membership have been lost or are unavailable.
4. *Reinstatement.*

Section C—Termination of Membership. Membership shall be terminated for any of the following reasons:

1. *Death.*
2. *Resignation.* Only written resignations shall be considered. The person resigning shall not be dropped from membership until the matter of resignation has been discussed with the member and accepted by the church.
3. *Transfer.* A member wishing to unite with another church may have a letter of transfer sent to that church stating his current standing in the church. He shall remain a responsibility of this church until he is accepted into the new church membership.
4. *Failure to Maintain Qualification.* If, in the opinion of the council, a member fails to maintain qualification for membership, the council shall follow Matthew 18: 15-20 in an effort to gain his renewed commitment. Failing this, he shall by resolution of the council be placed on an inactive membership list and lose his privilege of voting. The council shall continue to seek his renewed commitment for a period of one year, after which he shall be dropped from membership by vote of the church.
5. *Detrimental Conduct.* Any member or officer whose conduct is detrimental to the good of the church, provided the council feels action is necessary, shall, in accord with Matthew 18:15-20, be invited to meet with the council to explain his actions. Mindful that the purpose of this paragraph is understanding and reconciliation, every effort shall be made to resolve the matter at this time. If it is not resolved, the council may by a two-thirds vote of its total membership recommend to the church that the member be removed from office and/or dropped from church membership. To be adopted, the recommendation of the council must have a two-thirds vote of the church members present, qualified, and voting at any business meeting, provided the entire voting membership of the church has been notified in writing naming the person against whom the action is proposed at least one week in advance of the meeting, and provided the person in question is given an opportunity to speak on his own behalf before the vote is taken. Any member dropped from membership under this paragraph shall not be

reinstated without the recommendation of the council and the vote of the church.

ARTICLE V—OFFICERS

Section A—Qualifications. Each officer shall
1. be an active member of this church,
2. not hold more than one position on the officer level,
3. attend the regular council meetings and church business meetings,
4. carry out to the best of his ability the functions of his office as defined in this constitution and the bylaws.

Section B—Election and Term. Each officer shall be elected by majority vote of those present, qualified and voting at the annual meeting of the church, for a term of three years. Terms shall be staggered so that a third of the officers are elected each year, one of whom each year shall be the moderator, the clerk, or the treasurer. Officers shall serve until their successors are elected. No officer shall succeed himself in office except the clerk, treasurer, and financial secretary, who may serve a maximum of two consecutive terms. If any office becomes vacant in mid-term, the church shall elect a successor to fulfill the unexpired term.

Section C—Titles and Duties. All officers shall submit a written report to the church annually, and make progress reports from time to time as the church or moderator may require. By resolution, the church may assign to any office such other duties as may be required. All officers, in consultation with the pastor and moderator, may appoint such persons or committees as may be necessary to assist them in carrying out their responsibilities. All officers shall be accountable to the council and to the church membership, and shall transfer to their successors (or assigns) all records pertaining to their offices. (Accountability and responsibility is further defined under Article VII, Section B.)

Paragraph 1. *The moderator* shall
a. preside at business meetings of the church;
b. serve as chairman of the church council;
c. cooperate with the pastor in coordinating the work of officers, committees, and organizations of the church;
d. have the privilege of ex officio membership in all committees and organizations of the church;
e. appoint the following, subject to the approval of the council:
   (1) the nominating committee,
   (2) auditor (or auditing committee),
   (3) delegates to organizations with which the church is affiliated,
   (4) special committees

Paragraph 2. *The clerk* shall

a. keep minutes of all business sessions of the church;
b. serve as secretary of the church council;
c. maintain a permanent and current record of both active and inactive members, including dates and manner of admission, change of status (active or inactive), and dismissal;
d. write for and issue letters of dismissal and recommendation;
e. maintain (in addition to the church office file) a file of annual reports, booklets, and other documents of historical significance.

Paragraph 3. *The treasurer* shall

a. have custody of all church funds and securities;
b. make necessary disbursements of monies by check;
c. maintain an accurate record of receipts and disbursements as approved by the council;
d. maintain such separate and/or accruing accounts as the church or council may direct with the current balance for each;
e. be ready at any time upon reasonable notice, but especially at the regular meetings of the council, to furnish information concerning the financial condition of the church; and submit a written report to the council at least quarterly.

Paragraph 4. *The financial secretary* shall

a. count, record, and deposit all receipts of the church;
b. deliver to the treasurer deposit slips showing amounts to be credited to each fund which the church maintains;
c. keep a record of each individual's pledge and contributions, sending out a quarterly statement of the same to each individual;
d. furnish a written quarterly report to the church council, showing the number of paid and unpaid pledges.

Paragraph 5. *The stewardship councilman* shall be responsible for

a. the conducting of an annual church planning conference;
b. the development of a proposed budget for each calendar year from the requests of various departments of the church;
c. the conducting of an annual every member canvas (EMC)
   (1) to inform every family about the work of the church,
   (2) to promote percentage giving with 10 percent (a tithe) as the point of departure,
   (3) to obtain individual pledges toward the underwriting of the proposed budget;
d. adjusting the proposed budget to pledges received, for review by the council before presentation to the annual meeting of the church for adoption;

e. visiting every person who joins the church after the EMC is completed, as soon as possible after the person joins, in order to accomplish the three objectives of the EMC stated above;

f. year-round stewardship education

Paragraph 6. *The property councilman* shall be responsible for

a. maintaining and improving buildings, grounds, and all equipment which serves the buildings and grounds;

b. obtaining bids and letting contracts for necessary work on the property;

c. hiring and supervising custodial staff;

d. supervising volunteer work parties for jobs beyond the duties of the custodial staff;

e. in the event of a major building program, he shall serve on the building committee.

Paragraph 7. *The evangelism councilman* shall

a. in cooperation with the pastor, maintain an up-to-date list of prospective members;

b. in cooperation with the parish zone councilman, work out and maintain an effective year-round program for cultivation of the prospective members;

c. be responsible for the conducting of an annual one-week visitation evangelism program in which
   (1) every member of the church will be challenged to participate, and
   (2) an effort will be made to visit every prospective member in his own home to give him the opportunity to decide to follow Jesus or rededicate himself to following Jesus and to join this church;

d. in cooperation with the pastor, arrange for such other evangelistic programs as he may feel appropriate.

Paragraph 8. *The parish zone councilman* shall

a. divide the parish into an appropriate number of geographical zones;

b. in consultation with the pastor and moderator, select a leader to have the title of deacon (man or woman) for each zone, in accord with Acts 6:1-6, to serve for a period of four years, their terms being staggered—the parish zone councilman shall be deacon-at-large for the duration of his office;

c. in consultation with his deacons, develop a plan for
   (1) caring for the members of the church, especially those facing crises,
   (2) integrating new members into the life and fellowship of the church,
   (3) effective communication within the fellowship, both for emer-

gencies and to enhance the life of the church

Paragraph 9. *The mission councilman* shall

a. develop a year-round program designed to increase annually the church's support of the American Baptist World Mission;

b. in cooperation with the pastor, discover local community needs and develop and conduct programs through which the church can help to alleviate these needs, either unilaterally or in cooperation with other churches or agencies;

c. in the event of state, national, or world emergencies, develop and conduct relevant programs.

Paragraph 10. *The worship councilman* shall be responsible for

a. the music program of the church, including the appointment or hiring of the organist and choir director;

b. the appointment and training of ushers;

c. arrangements for the ordinances of Baptism and Communion;

d. the general decor of the sanctuary, including provision for flowers;

e. obtaining guest preachers in the absence of the pastor.

Paragraph 11. *The Christian education councilman* shall

a. provide for a graded church school, serving as its superintendent, appointing assistant or department superintendents as needed;

b. promote the effective use of American Baptist curriculum materials;

c. make annual provision for leadership training;

d. provide for youth programs, including the promotion of attendance at American Baptist camps, youth rallies, and conventions; and

e. provide for such other Christian education experiences as may be appropriate.

Paragraph 12. *The Women's Christian Fellowship (WCF) councilman* shall

a. be the WCF president as elected by that fellowship;

b. seek to coordinate the WCF program as an integral part of the total church program.

ARTICLE VI—THE PASTOR

Section A—Qualifications. The pastor shall

1. be a member in good standing in this church;

2. be committed to the American Baptist Convention fellowship;

3. meet the qualifications for ordination currently in force in the American Baptist Convention, the Pennsylvania Baptist Convention, and the Pittsburgh Baptist Association;

4. be ordained;

5. adhere to the Minister's Code of Ethics of the American Baptist Ministers Council.

Section B—Administrative Responsibility. The pastor shall be the chief executive officer of the church, and may act for the church between meetings of the council and business meetings of the church, provided such action is within the spirit of this constitution and within the spirit of current action by the church and council. The pastor shall cooperate with the moderator in coordinating the church's total program. He shall have the privilege of ex officio membership (without vote) in all committees and organizations of the church, and full membership (with vote) in the council. He shall be accountable to the council and church membership.

Section C—Pastoral Responsibilities. The pastor shall

1. prepare and conduct all public worship services unless other arrangements are made through the worship councilman;
2. call on and/or counsel those who are facing personal crises, especially those who are hospitalized or confined;
3. inspire and motivate the church to fulfill its purpose as stated in Article III.

Section D—Termination of Service.

Paragraph 1. *Resignation.* The pastor may resign giving one month's notice.

Paragraph 2. *Dismissal.* The church shall seek to avoid dismissing its pastor by working out an alternate agreement with him. Failing this, the church may dismiss the pastor only in accordance with Article IV, Section C, Paragraph 5.

ARTICLE VII—COUNCIL

Section A—Constituency. The council shall consist of the officers of the church as listed under Article V, Section C, and the pastor.

Section B—Responsibilities. The council shall be the executive body of the church, acting for the church when the church is not in business session, provided such action is within the spirit of this constitution and within the spirit of current action of the church. (The council shall have such powers and responsibilities as normally held by boards of deacons, deaconesses, trustees, and Christian education in American Baptist churches.) The council shall be accountable to the church membership and report at all business meetings of the church. In addition to the responsibilities assigned to specific officers in Article V, Section C, which are council responsibilities delegated to the specific officers, the council shall meet monthly to

1. Review, approve, and coordinate the work of all officers and their committees;
2. appoint such special and standing committees as may be necessary, in addition to those already provided for in this constitution, assigning them to a specific officer in the council;
3. review all matters which are to be brought before the church membership for action;
4. implement the action which the church takes in its business sessions;
5. authorize expenditures in keeping with the Annual Budget.
   a. In an emergency, an expenditure not to exceed $500 may be made by the council without first obtaining church approval.
   b. The council shall not buy, mortgage, lease, or transfer any real estate property without specific authorization by the church membership.

Section C—Quorum. Eight council members shall constitute a quorum.

ARTICLE VIII—COMMITTEES

Every committee of the church shall be answerable to a specific council member, normally, the council member appointing the committee. Committees appointed by the council at large and not specifically assigned to another council member shall be answerable to the moderator. Committees shall report to the council through their council member, but at the discretion of the council member and the moderator, one or more members of the committee may be invited to a council meeting to report in person.

ARTICLE IX—PULPIT COMMITTEE

Section A—Size and Election. When a pastor is to be sought, a pulpit committee consisting of not less than three nor more than seven active members of the church, shall be nominated by the church council and elected by the church.

Section B—Procedure. The pulpit committee shall
1. select a chairman and secretary;
2. seek the guidance and counsel of the executive secretary of the Pittsburgh Baptist Association;
3. secure an interim pastor;
4. make an analysis of the church's needs;
5. secure names and records of candidates;
6. reduce the list on the basis of written information available;
7. visit the candidates most likely to fulfill the needs of the church;

8. select one candidate at a time for recommendation to the church and arrange an opportunity for the church members to hear and meet him and for him to visit the community;
9. keep the church informed of progress with not less than a monthly report, but at the same time exercise discretion concerning confidential information about specific candidates.

Section C—Call. When the pulpit committee is agreed upon a candidate,

1. a pastor-church agreement shall be drawn up jointly by the pulpit committee and the candidate in writing including statements on
   a. the date the relationship is to begin,
   b. the starting salary and allowances,
   c. provision for salary and/or allowance increases,
   d. vacation,
   e. continuing education of the pastor for maintaining effective pastoral leadership, and
   f. preservation of denominational loyalty;
2. *The call* shall be extended by a two-thirds vote of members present, qualified, and voting at any regular or special business meeting of the church. The call shall be extended and accepted by a signed pastor-church agreement, one copy to be retained by the church clerk and the other copy forwarded to the pastor-elect. When the call is accepted, the pulpit committee shall be discharged.

ARTICLE X—CHURCH MEETINGS

Section A—Public Meetings. Public services for worship shall be held each Sunday, and Communion (the Lord's Supper) celebrated monthly, normally on the first Sunday of each month. Occasional and other public meetings for worship, celebration, or study may be scheduled by the pastor, the council, or by majority vote of the church.

Section B—Business Meetings.

Paragraph 1. *The annual meeting* of the church shall be held on the second Sunday of January.

Paragraph 2. *Quarterly business meetings* shall be held in April, July, and October, the specific time and place to be set by the council or by vote of the church.

Paragraph 3. *Special business meetings* may be called at any time by the pastor; the moderator, or, upon the receipt of a petition of five members of the church from five different families, by the clerk.

Paragraph 4. *Notice* of the time, place, and object of all business meetings of the church shall be given at least one week in advance by verbal announcement from the pulpit at a regular public worship service, by written announcement in the Sunday bulletin, or by means of a mailing sent to all members.

Paragraph 5. Fifteen percent of the active members of the church shall be required to conduct business, and only active members of the church shall have the privilege of voting.

Paragraph 6. *Parliamentary authority* for the conduct of business meetings shall be *Robert's Rules of Order Revised,* where they are not inconsistent with this constitution.

ARTICLE XI—AMENDMENTS

Amendments to this constitution may be made at any regular or special business meeting of the church by a two-thirds vote of those present, qualified, and voting, provided that the proposed amendments have been presented in writing at a previous business meeting of the church and distributed to all active members at least four weeks before action is taken by the church.

ARTICLE XII—BYLAWS

In the event that this constitution needs clarification short of an amendment, or if in the ongoing experience of the church, it finds a practice or procedure effective, these may be formulated as bylaws, which shall be adopted, amended or deleted by simple majority vote at any business meeting of the church, provided they are not in conflict with the constitution.

EXHIBIT 3-C

CHURCH MEMBERSHIP

Pastor	Church Council

Moderator	Clerk	Treasurer	Financial Sec.	Property	Steward-ship	Worship	Christian Ed.	Parish Zone	Evangelism	Mission	Women
Pastoral Relations				Church Bldg.	Planning	Music	Ch. School		Advertising	Offerings	Interpretation
Pulpit Supply				Education Bldg.	Conf.	Ushers	Youth Groups		Canvassing	Mission Ed.	Missions
				Manse	EMC	Decor			Visitation	Projects	Service
				Grounds	Steward-ship Ed.	Ordinances			Evangel. Crusades		Kitchen
											Auxiliaries

The Church Council consists of twelve persons with every person having a specific assignment for which he is responsible, but in council all take (or share) responsibility for the welfare of the whole church. Each member of the council may take care of his tasks himself, or delegate them to stewards of his choice, who would become his committee, with the council member as chairman.

The Parish Zone Plan would divide the parish geographically, with a pastoral assistance (deacon) as the leader of each zone, responsible for (1) watch-care over the members in his zone (2) notifying the pastor in cases requiring his attention, (3) cultivating new families in his zone, and (4) notifying his constituents in cases of special events or emergencies (telephone tree). Meetings could be held within the zones at the discretion of initiative of the zone leader for such things as Bible study, prayer, getting acquainted, or projects of service and outreach. The zone leaders would be key persons in pastoral care and could appropriately be used by the worship chairman (or ordinances steward) to serve on Communion Sundays.

67

EXHIBIT 3-D

AMERICAN BAPTIST CHURCHES OF
PENNSYLVANIA AND DELAWARE

CONSTITUTION

The following constitution and bylaws of the newly formed American Baptist Churches of Pennsylvania and Delaware were adopted by the convening delegates of both states on Saturday, October 28, 1972, at State College, Pa. There are some changes involved which make these documents differ from the proposed constitution and bylaws which were printed in the June 1972 issue of this journal.

ARTICLE I

Name: The name of this organization shall be the American Baptist Churches of Pennsylvania and Delaware, hereafter referred to as the Region.

ARTICLE II

Denominational Relationships: The organization shall be affiliated with the American Baptist Churches in the USA as a Region and shall cooperate with it in the support of denominational activities. It shall provide a means by which the membership may communicate with the American Baptist Churches in the USA.

This organization accepts the Statement of Purpose adopted by the American Baptist Convention in Seattle in May, 1969, as its underlying basis of thought and practice.*

The American Baptist Churches in the USA, as a manifestation of the church universal, bears witness to God's intention to bring redemption and wholeness to all creation. American Baptists believe that God's intention* can be sought and followed in local congregations and other gatherings of Christians and in associational, regional, national, and world bodies as they receive from one another mutual counsel and correction. Since Jesus Christ is the head of the Church, each body of Christians seeking to order its life in accordance with the Scriptures under the guidance of the Holy Spirit has a proper responsibility under God for maintaining its life of worship, witness, and ministry.

* Statement of Purpose of the American Baptist Churches in the USA.

In every area of their common life, American Baptists, acknowledging the importance of creative diversity, seek such a balance of freedom and order as will keep all parts of the Convention open to the guidance of the Holy Spirit and at the same time enable them to work responsibly to carry out the common task of mission and ministry in our time.

The American Baptist Churches in the USA acknowledges that it shares a common faith in Christ with churches which may be quite different from it in history, polity and practice. Consequently, it seeks to share with them a common ministry and to express it faithfully.

The American Baptist Churches in the USA further acknowledges that God's will is also manifested in movements outside the formal structures of Christ's church, and that, therefore, it must respond faithfully to such disclosures.

In light of this affirmation, the following in the form of a statement of purpose of the American Baptist Churches in the USA is intended to implement and not to alter the objects of the corporation as stated in the Act of Incorporation:

—to bear witness to the Gospel of Jesus Christ in the world and to lead persons to Christ;

—to seek the mind of Christ on moral, spiritual, political, economic, social, denominational, and ecumenical matters, and to express to the rest of society on behalf of American Baptists their convictions as to the mind of Christ in these matters;

—to guide, unify, and assist American Baptists in their witness in the world, in preparing members for the work of ministry, and in serving both those within and outside the fellowship of Christ;

—and to promote closer relations among American Baptist churches and groups, within the whole Body of Christ and to promote understanding with other religious bodies.

ARTICLE III

Purpose:

(I) To provide an organization through which the member churches can implement and fulfill their role as part of the church of Jesus Christ.

(II) To implement as an organization its corporate responsibility for that mission of the church which extends beyond the local congregation and related units;

1. To support the American Baptist Churches in the USA in its world mission;

2. To extend the total mission of the church throughout the Pennsylvania and Delaware region;
3. To engage in such acts of charity and to establish and support such institutions as shall give effective expression of the Christian concern of the membership for the needs of persons;
4. To provide the corporate structures by which the membership can give effective expression of Christian concern for the needs of society;
5. To develop in all persons an awareness and appreciation that God is Creator and Source of all so that stewardship is fulfilled.

ARTICLE IV

Membership: The constituency of the Region shall be those churches and fellowship groups which cooperate in its work, and are eligible for membership in the American Baptist Churches in the USA.

ARTICLE V

Meetings: The organization shall meet at such times and places as shall be provided for in the Bylaws. Representation of the churches at such meetings shall be fair and proportionate.

ARTICLE VI

Regional Board: The business of the organization between meetings of members shall be conducted by a board known as the Regional Board. This Board is to be elected in such manner and is to have such powers and responsibilities as provided in the Bylaws.

ARTICLE VII

Officers of the Region: The officers of the Region shall be the President, Vice President, Recording Secretary, and Regional Executive Minister, and such other officers as may be elected or appointed from time to time.

ARTICLE VIII

Parliamentary Order: All meetings of the organization shall be governed by *Robert's Rules of Order* according to its latest authorized edition.

ARTICLE IX

Quorum: A quorum shall consist of fifty properly accredited delegates representing at least twenty-five churches, present at any meeting of which notice has been given as provided in the Bylaws.

ARTICLE X

Amendments: This Constitution may be amended by a two-thirds vote of the delegates present at any membership meeting, provided three months notice of the proposed change shall have been given in written form by mail to member churches.

BYLAWS

ARTICLE I
OFFICE

Section 1. The principal office shall be at Valley Forge, Pennsylvania.
Section 2. Other offices may be established by Regional Board action.

ARTICLE II
MEETING OF THE MEMBERSHIP

Section 1. The membership shall meet biennially on the alternate year of the American Baptist Churches in the USA biennial meeting in either the state of Delaware or the state of Pennsylvania at such time and place as may be determined by the Regional Board.

Section 2. Written notice shall be given at least sixty days prior to the biennial meeting in the monthly publication of the organization unless otherwise provided for in the Constitution or these Bylaws.

Section 3. A quorum shall consist of fifty properly accredited delegates representing at least twenty-five churches, present at any meeting of which notice has been given.

Section 4. The membership as provided for in Article IV of the Constitution shall be entitled to the following delegates at any biennial or special meeting of the organization.

(*a*) The member church shall be represented by:

Two delegates and one additional delegate for every one hundred resident members or major fraction thereof above the first hundred designated by any cooperating church from its own membership. However, the number of such delegates shall be subject to the following provision: The number of annual voting members or delegates designated by any church shall not exceed a number bearing the same ratio to the maximum number permitted by the foregoing provisions of this section that the amount of benevolence funds given by or through such church during the preceding fiscal year to the financial objectives adopted by the American Baptist Churches in the USA bears to the total benevolence funds given by and through the same

71

church during the same period. Fractional numbers of delegates shall be counted as one.

(b) An American Baptist Fellowship Group shall be recognized upon favorable action of the Executive Committee, and shall be represented by one delegate.

(c) The officers of the organization shall be ex officio delegates at all membership meetings. The regional professional staff employed by the Regional Board shall also be ex officio delegates to the membership meetings.

(d) At all membership meetings each delegate shall be entitled to one vote.

Section 5. A registration fee in the amount to be determined by the Regional Board, payable upon the presentation of credentials, shall be collected from all delegates, in return for which the printed reports of the Biennial Meeting and a copy of the Regional Bi-Annual shall be delivered to each accredited delegate without further cost. Offerings shall be received at the Biennial Meeting to aid in defraying the expenses thereof.

Section 6. Special meetings of the organization may be called by the Executive Minister at the request of the Regional Board, or by the Executive Committee, or by the Region's churches upon the written request of 10 percent or more of such churches, stating the time, place, and purpose of the meeting.

ARTICLE III
REGIONAL BOARD

Section 1. Members. These General Officers: President, Vice President, Recording Secretary, and the Regional Executive Minister.

General Members. One from each Association, with one additional member for each 10,000 members or fraction thereof above the first 10,000; three each from American Baptist Men of Pennsylvania and Delaware, American Baptist Women of Pennsylvania and Delaware, American Baptist Ministers Council of Pennsylvania and Delaware, and three to be nominated by the Regional Youth Committee; Executive Minister of the Philadelphia Baptist Association; Executive Minister of the Pittsburgh Baptist Association; immediate past president of the Region; twelve (12) Members-at-Large.

Section 2. Election. The general officers (other than the Regional Executive Minister), the Association members, the at-large members and the representatives of the American Baptist Men of Pennsylvania and Delaware, American Baptist Women of Pennsylvania and Delaware, American Baptist Ministers Council of Pennsylvania and Delaware, and the representatives of the Regional Youth Committee shall be elected at the biennial general meeting. Board members shall be elected for a two-year term and shall be eligible for two additional successive terms. The initial Regional Board shall be composed of one class of one-third which shall be elected for one term not to succeed itself, one class of one-third eligible for re-election for one additional term, and one class of one-third eligible for re-election to two additional terms.

Section 3. Rotation of Members. Association Members on the Regional Board should be proportionately balanced among lay women, lay men and clergy. To insure a balanced membership the Regional Executive Minister (in a given biennium) shall notify each Association of the category from which its nominee should be selected, namely lay women, lay men and clergy. Through the members-at-large category the Nominating Committee should seek to balance the membership in terms of age, skill, ethnic and language groups.

Section 4. Officers. The general officers of the Region shall be the officers of the Regional Board.

Section 5. Qualifications. The officers and members of the Regional Board shall be members of cooperating American Baptist churches or fellowship groups of the Region. No member or spouse of the Region or City Societies administrative unit's staff shall be eligible, except as provided in Article III, Section 1.

Section 6. Quorum. At each meeting of the Regional Board the majority of those persons then constituting the Board, present in person, shall constitute a quorum. If at any meeting there shall be no quorum present, the members present shall have power to adjourn the meeting from time to time, until a quorum is present and no notice of any such adjourned meeting need be given. At all meetings of the Regional Board each member shall be entitled to one vote. The majority vote of the members present and constituting a quorum shall determine the vote of the Regional Board.

Section 7. Absentees. Absence of a member from two consecutive meetings of the Board, without sufficient excuse, shall create a vacancy. In the event such vacancy occurs, the Executive Committee, in consultation with the association or program division whose representative is affected, shall be empowered to fill the vacancy until the next election by the Region.

Section 8. Time and Place of Meetings. The Regional Board shall hold (1) at least two meetings annually at the times and places fixed by the Board, (2) such regular or special meetings at such times and places as the Board may determine. The time and place of each regular or special meeting and the purpose of each special meeting shall be set forth in the notice of such meeting which shall be mailed by the Regional Recording Secretary to all members of the Regional Board not less than ten (10) nor more than forty

73

(40) days before the meeting. Special meetings of the Regional Board may be called at any time by the President or in his absence by the Vice President, and may be called upon the written request of ten percent of the members of the Regional Board delivered to the Regional Executive Minister.

Section 9. Functions. The Regional Board shall manage the affairs of the Region and, as part thereof, shall:

(a) give general oversight and direction to the life of the Region and its mission;

(b) determine policy in the areas of program assignment, planning, coordination and evaluation;

(c) establish and elect or appoint members or officers of such committees of the Regional Board, Divisions, Task Forces and other bodies, in the manner provided in these bylaws;

(d) elect the chairmen of the Program Divisions;

(e) define additional duties and powers of officers, divisions, committees, commissions and task forces not otherwise provided for;

(f) adopt such procedures as it may deem proper concerning the appointment or removal of officers and agents, and fix their compensation by the Region, and direct and instruct them concerning their respective duties;

(g) adopt such procedures as it may deem proper, including those for the control, management, acquisition and disposition of the real and personal property of the Region;

(h) prepare and recommend to the biennial meeting of the Region a budget necessary for the operation thereof; (i) give leadership to the people and churches of the Region by formulating statements and instituting programs that speak to particular issues confronting them;

(i) give leadership to the people and churches of the Region by formulating statements and instituting programs that speak to particular issues confronting them;

(j) determine which matters may be voted by mail as well as at the time of meeting;

(k) adopt such regulations as it may deem proper for the conduct of its affairs, all provided, however, that such action shall not be inconsistent with the organization's Act of Incorporation, the constitution or these bylaws; and

(l) publish and distribute to the membership an annual Financial and Progress Report.

(m) elect the Regional Executive Minister.

ARTICLE IV
OFFICERS

Section 1. The general officers of the Region shall be the President, Vice President, Recording Secretary, and the Regional Executive Minister.

Section 2. Upon nomination of the Regional Nominating Committee, the President and the Vice President of the Region shall be elected by the delegates at their biennial meeting for a single two-year term only. The office of President shall rotate among lay women, lay men and clergy.

Section 3. Duties of the President. The President of the Region shall be an ex officio member of all standing committees of the Regional Board and of all committees of the Region, and shall also:

(a) preside at the meetings of the delegates, and at the meetings of the Regional Board and the Executive Committee thereof at which he shall be present;

(b) in consultation with the Executive Minister,

(i) appoint members and the chairman of the Biennial Program Committee and such other committees (other than committees of the Regional Board) as may be required for the work of the Region;

(ii) make recommendations to the Regional Board on matters of importance to the mission of the Region;

(iii) perform such other duties as the Regional Board may assign to him.

Section 4. Duties of the Vice President. The Vice President shall discharge such functions as may be assigned to him by the President or by the Regional Board, In the absence of the President he shall serve as the acting President and shall preside at all meetings at which the President should preside under these Bylaws. The Vice President when serving as President shall be an ex officio member of all committees of the Regional Board.

Section 5. Recording Secretary. Upon the nomination of the Regional Nominating Committee the Regional Biennial delegates shall elect a Recording Secretary for a term of two years. Subject to the direction and supervision of the Executive Minister he shall discharge the usual duties of a corporate secretary, including the keeping of true minutes of meetings of the delegates, the Regional Board and its Executive Committee.

Section 6. Executive Minister. Upon nomination by the Regional Executive Committee, the Executive Minister shall be elected by the Regional Board to serve at its pleasure. Subject to the general direction and supervision of the Regional Board, the Executive Minister shall be the chief executive officer of the Region and shall be responsible for the day by day administration of its affairs and of its staff. He shall have power, subject to the approval of the Regional Board, to execute legal instruments on behalf of the Region. He shall have such additional duties as the Regional Board may prescribe.

Section 7. Professional Staff. Upon nomination by the Regional Executive Committee, the Professional Staff shall be elected by the Regional Board to serve at its pleasure. Subject to the general direction and supervision of the Executive Minister and the Regional Board, the Professional Staff shall be responsible for those duties assigned by the Board.

Section 8. Treasurer. The Treasurer shall be a member of the Professional Staff of the Region. Subject to the direction and supervision of the Executive Minister, the Treasurer shall arrange for the maintenance, safekeeping, disposition and disbursement of the funds and securities of the Region. He shall deposit the funds of the Region in such banks, savings institutions or trust companies or in such vault or vaults as may from time to time be designated by the Regional Board. The withdrawal of such funds or the transfer of such securities shall be made only on the written authorization of two or more of the members of the Regional Board, officers, or employees of the Region as may be designated from time to time by the Regional Board for such purpose. The Treasurer shall give a bond for the faithful discharge of his duties in such sum, and with such surety, as the Regional Board shall require. He shall account for and report regularly to the Region at its meetings and to the meetings of the Regional Board subject to audit.

Section 9. Removal of Officers. The Executive Minister of the Region may be removed from office, with or without stated cause, by the affirmative vote of at least two-thirds (2/3) of the members of the Regional Board. The President, the Vice President, and the Recording Secretary of the Region may be removed, with or without stated cause, by a majority vote of the delegates duly convened at a regular or special meeting. The Regional Board, by the affirmative vote of at least two-thirds (2/3) of the members of the Regional Board, may suspend, for stated cause and for such period as it deems suitable, the authority of the President, the Vice President, and the Recording Secretary.

ARTICLE V
COMMITTEES OF THE REGIONAL BOARD

Section 1. Standing or Special Committees. By resolution adopted by a majority of the Regional Board, the Regional Board shall designate its standing or special committees each consisting of three or more members of the Board. Each such committee shall have such powers as may from time to time be set forth in these Bylaws or in a resolution of the Regional Board, provided that no such committee shall have authority as to matters as are specified by the laws of the Commonwealth of Pennsylvania to pertain exclusively to the jurisdiction of the entire Regional Board. The Regional Board may designate one or more of its members as alternate members of any standing committee, who may replace any absent member or members at any meeting of such committee.

   (a) Vacancies—A vacancy in the membership of any standing committee or a special committee of the Regional Board may be filled for the balance of the term by a majority vote of the Regional Board at any meeting upon nomination of the Regional Board Nominating Committee.

   (b) Rules of Procedure—Each Committee of the Regional Board shall fix its own rules of procedure, and except as otherwise provided in the Bylaws, shall be chaired by a person designated by the Regional Board.

Section 2. Executive Committee. Between meetings of the Regional Board the Executive Committee shall have such authority of the Regional Board as such Board shall from time to time specify by resolution adopted by such Board. The Executive Committee shall meet at regular intervals as specified by the Regional Board and on special occasions upon the call of not less than five (5) days' notice by the President or any three (3) members of the Committee. In addition to such other functions that may be assigned to the Executive Committee by the Regional Board from time to time, the Executive Committee shall select and recommend to the Regional Board a person to serve as Executive Minister of the Region and shall evaluate the work of, and assign program functions to, the related program divisions. The Executive Committee shall be the Personnel Committee of the Regional Board.

   (a) Membership of the Executive Committee—The Executive Committee shall consist of:

     —one member from among the members-at-large of the Regional Board to be appointed by the President.

     —the chairman of each program division

     —the President, Vice President, Recording Secretary, and the Executive Minister of the Region

     —the immediate past President

     The President or in his absence the Vice President of the Region shall be the chairman of the Committee.

   (b) Action of the Executive Committee—At each meeting of the Executive Committee a majority of those persons then constituting the Committee, present in person, shall constitute a quorum. At all meetings of the Executive Committee each person thereof shall be entitled to one vote. The majority vote of the members of the Executive Committee present and constituting a quorum shall determine the vote of the Executive Committee. The Executive Committee shall maintain a record of all of its acts and proceedings which shall be made available to members of the Regional Board no later than at their next meeting.

Section 3. Regional Board Nominating Committee. The Executive Committee shall appoint three (3) of its members to serve as the Regional Board Nominating Committee. This committee shall nominate the chairman and members of the Divisions and Committees of the Regional Board. The Committee members shall serve for one biennium.

ARTICLE VI
COMMITTEES OF THE AMERICAN BAPTIST CHURCHES OF PENNSYLVANIA AND DELAWARE

Section 1. *Nominating Committee.*

(a) There shall be a Nominating Committee of the Region consisting of the following members:

—One member from each group: American Baptist Men of Pennsylvania and Delaware, American Baptist Women of Pennsylvania and Delaware, American Baptist Ministers Council of Pennsylvania and Delaware, to be named by their respective organizations; and a youth appointed by the Regional Youth Committee;

—Two members at large from the membership of the Region nominated by the Nominating Committee of the Regional Board and elected by the Executive Committee;

—One member from each association.

(b) The Nominating Committee shall be staffed by the Executive Minister or someone appointed by him.

(c) The chairman shall be appointed from among the members of the Committee by the President of the Region.

(d) The Nominating Committee shall have an Executive Committee from its own membership and composed of its chairman, the two members-at-large, two representatives from the program divisions, and three representatives from the associations. The members shall be appointed by the President, and shall expedite the work of the Nominating Committee.

(e) The chairman shall convene the Executive Committee and the Nominating Committee at least three months prior to the membership meeting of the Region.

(*f*) The consent of all nominees shall be secured before being presented as candidates for election either by prepared ballot or upon nomination from the floor.

(*g*) The report of the Nominating Committee shall be presented to the Region on the first full day of its biennial meeting. At least one full session shall intervene between the presentation of the report and the election of officers.

Section 2. Biennial Meeting Program Committee. There shall be a Program Committee with responsibility for detailing the plans with respect to the program of the Biennial Meetings of the delegates. A committee of not less than seven (7) persons shall be appointed by the President in consultation with the Executive Minister, subject to approval by the Regional Board. The President and the Executive Minister shall serve as ex officio members of the Committee. The Regional Board may assign such specific functions to the committee as it deems appropriate.

Section 3. Statement of Concern Committee. There shall be a Statement of Concern Committee of the Region. The Committee shall consist of not less than seven (7) persons who shall be representative of the constituency of the cooperating churches, including clergy, laymen, laywomen, youth and representatives of minority groups in the Region, and shall be elected by the delegates at their biennial meeting upon nomination by the Nominating Committee. No member shall be eligible to serve more than three consecutive two-year terms. The chairman shall be elected by the members of the Committee from among their members. A vacancy in the membership of the Committee occurring between biennial meetings of the delegates shall be filled by the President upon the recommendation of the Executive Committee for the remainder of the term vacated.

The functions of the Committee shall be prescribed by the Regional Board and shall include the preparation of such background and other materials, including statements for consideration and adoption, as may be necessary or desirable in order to enable the meetings of the Regional Board and the delegates to make the maximum contribution to the fulfillment of the purpose and mission of the Region. One member of the professional staff shall be assigned to work with the Committee.

ARTICLE VII
PROGRAM DIVISIONS

Section 1. The program priorities established by the Regional Board shall be implemented through the work of the Program Divisions which this Board shall create. The Regional Board shall be responsible for establishing the necessary Program Divisions other than those with American Baptist Churches in the USA counterparts. The Divisions shall be accountable to the Regional Board and shall make periodic reports to this body.

Section 2. The chairman of each Division shall be elected by the Regional Board upon nomination by the Regional Board's Nominating Committee and shall serve on the Executive Committee of the Region.

Section 3. The members of the Regional Board shall be elected to a Program Division by the Executive Committee upon nomination of the Regional Board Nominating Committee in consultation with the Executive Minister and the Chairman of the Division. The size and assignment of each division will be determined by the Executive Committee as deemed necessary to accomplish the goals and objectives of the Region adopted for that current biennium.

Section 4. The Vice Chairman shall be elected by the members of each division and shall be eligible to serve on the Executive Committee in the absence of the Chairman of the Division.

Section 5. Organizations such as the American Baptist Women of Pennsylvania and Delaware (ABWPD), American Baptist Men of Pennsylvania and Delaware (ABMPD), American Baptist Ministers Council of Pennsylvania and Delaware (ABMCPD), shall work in cooperation with their American Baptist Churches in the USA counterparts. These regional organizations shall constitute Program Divisions. The members of the Regional Board representing the various organizations (ABWPD, ABMPD, ABMCPD) shall be elected to the proper corresponding program divisions, and one person from each division shall serve on the Executive Committee.

Section 6. The Program Divisions may add such non-compensated consultants as may be required to provide specialized assistance in their work. Such consultants shall serve as advisors to the divisions rather than as members.

ARTICLE VIII
MISCELLANEOUS

Section 1. Instruments. All checks, drafts, orders, notes, deeds, security instruments, powers and other legal instruments shall be executed on behalf of the American Baptist Churches of Pennsylvania and Delaware by such person or persons and in such manner as the Regional Board may direct by resolution.

Section 2. Seal. The corporate seal of the American Baptist Churches of Pennsylvania and Delaware shall be in such form as may be determined by the Regional Board.

Section 3. Notices. Whenever any notice is required to be given under the provisions of the laws of the Commonwealth of Pennsylvania or these Bylaws, a waiver thereof, in writing signed by the person or persons entitled to said notice, whether before or after the time stated therein, shall be deemed equivalent thereto.

Section 4. Fiscal Year. The fiscal year shall be the calendar year.

Section 5. Glossary of Terms. Task Force (Group)—a unit whose membership, task, and length of service shall be designated by the appointing group. Normally its task is achievable within a short period of time and is nonrecurring and is narrow in scope, versus that of a division.

Committee—is a unit more permanent in nature, with a more diverse task, whose membership shall be designated, including term of office when created.

Commission—is like a committee only its membership includes as voting members professional staff as well as those from the constituency.

Division—is a unit, with a permanent task, broad in scope, with ongoing responsibilities often broadly stated so the necessity for change is limited. Its membership is rotating in nature, composed of the constituency of the creating organization.

Ex officio—by virtue of an office, which carries with it the right to vote.

Fellowship Group—a group of Baptist Christians which meets for worship, fellowship and service supporting the American Baptist mission, which seeks separate recognition and representation in the Region.

American Baptist Churches in the USA (ABC, USA) Counterparts—those divisions which are similar in nature on a national level, such as American Baptist Men, American Baptist Women, and American Baptist Ministers Council.

Professional Staff—Executive Minister, Resource Ministers, Area Ministers, Administrative Assistant, Treasurer.

ARTICLE IX
AMENDMENTS

These Bylaws may be suspended, altered, or amended at any biennial or specially called meeting of the delegates of the Region for which written notice of the proposed change has been given at least thirty (30) days in advance. A majority vote of those present shall be required for adoption.

IV
Outreach

Wisdom is knowing what *to do next, skill is knowing* how *to do it, and virtue is the doing.*

Anonymous

In this chapter we will consider both Evangelism and Service to the community. There has probably been no more divisive area or subject within the church over the past twenty or thirty years than this subject. It really is a shame and disgrace that church leadership —clergy and laity—has so misunderstood, partly understood, and generally created divisions within the church and confusion without. We should be doing just the opposite. Some churches have overcome this basic problem—and are succeeding, proving that it can be done. We should learn from their experience and get on with the job before the church loses the opportunity completely.

Since the church must, of necessity, renew or replenish itself just to continue its existence, it would seem to be a practical necessity to have an evangelistic outreach. It is necessary to bring people into the church in order to have people to make up a church that has a social or service outreach. On the other hand, it is doubtful that the church can have an adequate environment for a successful evangelistic outreach if it is not demonstrating God's love to its fellowmen through servicing man's physical and mental needs where they are found in the local community.

In other words, totally aside from the spiritual teaching of the Bible, church leadership should be pragmatic enough to see that one form of outreach cannot be perpetuated long term without the other. More importantly, one who studies the Bible in any depth can hardly escape the teaching (yes, even the Commandment) that as Christians we must do both types of outreach.

How much of each must be done? How do you balance the two efforts in your own church? Only the local church can decide. The only real guideline is to balance your opportunity in the community with the capability of the people in your church. The planning process described elsewhere will help you to do this. The discussion that follows will be devoted to the basics of starting and maintaining both types of outreach efforts.

Evangelism

As defined here, evangelism refers to all those methods and efforts whose primary purpose is to persuade individual human beings to a belief and faith in Jesus Christ as the Son of God, as the Way to having our sins forgiven for a peaceful and joyful life now and throughout eternity. Also, it is an effort to enlist believers in study for growth and maturity, that we may make Christ the Lord of our lives through service to our fellowmen—"in as much as you have done it unto the least of these my brethren, you have done it unto me" (Matt. 25:40). There are many forms and methods. For our discussion, forms are grouped into three categories.

1. *Mass Evangelism*

Large groups of people are brought together at one place to hear one person "proclaim the Gospel." The number of people may vary from approximately 100 in a small church, where the "preaching" usually is done by a local pastor, to several hundred (also normally held in the local church, whose leader is a more prominent pastor or a less well known person serving as a full-time evangelist), or to many thousands gathered in a local auditorium or stadium, as made famous by Dr. Billy Graham.

This latter form of evangelism has had the longest historical usage and is perhaps best known. The key to its success is (*a*) good organization and advance planning, (*b*) effective use of modern communications and promotion methods to reach large segments of the population to interest them in coming together, and (c) an attractive personality and effective communicator to present the Gospel. The personality's reputation also serves as a "drawing power." Dr. Billy Graham and his team are most effective with the mass evangelism method. So much has been written about him and his methods that no attempt will be made even to summarize them here, but merely to refer those interested to their nearest bookstore.

A variation on this form is the use of radio and TV to reach people in their homes. We suspect that the use of radio and TV is vastly overrated as an evangelistic outreach method. Actually, it functions more as a "sustainer" of existing active church members. We do commend, however, to those interested in the mass media of radio and TV, study of the methods and techniques of the Reverend Oral Roberts of Tulsa, Oklahoma. Details of Roberts's ministry, too, are already well documented and will not be pursued here except to call attention to two points.

First, Roberts perhaps has no equal in the planning, preparation, and presentation of the Gospel message with the environment of his current-day audience in mind. Second, Roberts changes and adapts his methods as the environment changes without changing the basic message. Anyone watching his TV specials can hardly escape awareness of this. Just as we admiringly apply the term *pro* to someone who is the very best in athletics, politics, or theatrics, so Oral Roberts is a pro in evangelism, even though he is more frequently thought of for his healing or teaching ministry.

Being a pro is extremely important in evangelism and every area of church life for a very good reason. That reason relates to a fact of the environment in which all of us live. Practically all of the population in the United States is exposed to a high standard of professionalism as far as technique, method, and total performance are concerned. We are exposed through the medium of TV. We see the very best professional athletes, actors, and performers in every field right in our own living rooms. Consciously or unconsciously high performance standards (although not necessarily subject matter) are established in the minds of most people. Subsequently, we reject and then abandon the less than inspiring sermon, the ill-prepared church school teacher, and church programs which are poorly thought out and communicated.

Pastors and lay people need to learn the lesson that Oral Roberts's methods teach, and then apply them to all that they do—"Be a pro and see your effectiveness grow."

2. Small Group Evangelism

The church school is perhaps the best example of this general form, but is not limited to it. For many Protestant churches, the church (Sunday) school has been long known as the evangelistic arm of the church. It is well established that where Bible teaching precedes, evangelism has its greatest success; and where Bible teaching follows, evangelism has its most lasting effect. To be effective, class size must remain small (ten to thirty) so that there can be a personal relationship between the teacher and the pupil; and that relationship must include a deep concern and personal effort on the part of the teacher to "win" every member of the class and cause each member to be led to reach out to bring others in, that they, too, may be won and reproduce themselves as Christians. It is also necessary to have a spirit-led, and therefore prepared, teacher— again it is necessary to be a pro. If we are willing and really try to prepare, it is surprising how much of a pro God can make of us. Today, it is the poorly prepared and less than dedicated teachers that kill the church school, not the literature, although much of this is poorly done and falls far short of what is needed. The church school and Christian education are dealt with in greater detail in chapter six.

3. Personal Evangelism

There is no more effective way to communicate your faith and the love of God than in a one-to-one situation. This we believe to be one of the Biblical intents when we are taught that every Christian is to be a minister—to live and share our faith at work or play wherever we are. This is the spiritual maturity and end result to which most of the church program should be aimed.

How can you help your people learn personal evangelism? The answer is to set up a regular home visitation program. Many Protestant denominations, private organizations, and individuals have developed rather complete plans and methods for this purpose. Most follow the same basic principles of finding a prospect and then sending lay people out, two by two, to call in the home—to share their faith—and invite the prospect to make that decision necessary to meet his needs. All of these are adaptations of the first-century plan that Jesus Himself set up. A general outline of how to start such a program in your church follows.

The pessimist sees difficulty in every opportunity; the optimist opportunity in every difficulty.

L. P. Jocks

In order to start, it is necessary to become completely familiar with a program of proven effectiveness and to understand the need for it so that you can communicate the program to your people and demonstrate to them the real need. Two 1973 facts should help. Only 40 percent of the United States population now attend any church. The reasons are legion, but one important reason deals with the second fact. Approximately one out of every five families moves each year. We are a mobile society, which results in broken bonds of habit and friendships—the habit of church attendance, the persuasive influence of a friend or pastor that helped maintain the habit prior to moving. Also there are the competitive influences of ease of travel, recreation, and other activities. How many people do you personally know that own some form of mobile camping equipment? All these things, together with the lack of adaptation and unprofessional approach by our churches, are permitting large numbers of people to be lost from the church.

Religious Census

The first step is to locate the unchurched. Take a religious census. This can be done cooperatively with other churches in the area, or alone. A cooperative effort is preferred so that enough manpower is available to do an entire community each year. If done alone, it may be necessary to do a portion each year for three to five years before it is possible to repeat an area. Because of the mobility factor mentioned previously, this is undesirable.

How do you take a religious census? What questions do you ask? How much time does it take? What records do you keep? How do you plan it? When should it be done?

Sunday afternoon between 2:00 P.M. and 5:00 P.M. during the period of mid-January to mid-March has been found a most desirable time to schedule a religious census. More families will be

86

home and less involved with other things than any other day or time of year. Although the weather may be somewhat undesirable in parts of the country, experience and weather forecasts can be used to schedule with minimum disruption from severe weather. Of course, one of the reasons for scheduling during this period is that weather tends to keep more families at home. A census taker with fifteen minutes of training should be able to contact one home every two or three minutes on an urban or suburban street. Remember, this is a census to discover the unchurched, not a calling program to enlist the unchurched—calling follows later. A clipboard with a supply of the following forms and a pen or pencil are the only tools required.

STREET:					
House No.	Names	Est. Ages	Church Preference	Membership Where	Prospect?

The census taker should ring the doorbell or knock, then take one step back from the door when it is opened, and say, "I'm———; we're taking a religious census today. May I ask your church preference?" Should a child open the door, ask for the father or mother before asking the above question. In about forty-nine of fifty homes, there will be an immediate response, giving a denominational preference. If the people are active members of a local church, that information will be volunteered also. If they are members of a local church and actively attending, quickly say "Thank you very much; we are looking for the unchurched"; then move on to the next home. Do not visit. Do not enter the home when invited in, as you most frequently will be. Say, "Thank you very much, but this will only take a minute," and remain outside. It is too time consuming to go in—this is a census.

If the answer to church preference does not indicate local membership, then ask, "May I ask if your membership is in a church in this community or in another location where you have lived?" If membership is local, move on. If the individual is not a member, or if he is a member in some other location, determine if this answer applies to both husband and wife. These people then are obviously prospects for some local church. Subsequent calling will establish whether it is your church or whether you should refer them to another church. When you have determined that the people are unchurched locally, record their preference and the location of their membership if it is elsewhere, estimate the age of the parents and ask for the names and ages of the children, and then move on. Doing all of this should require no more than two or three minutes. In census taking, only one person goes to a door, even though they are working in teams of two. Each person works one side of a street. In doing so, each person involved can contact as many as thirty homes per hour, depending on the density of the neighborhood. Experience shows that a minimum of 10 percent, and up to 20 percent, of the homes will be prospects. With an average of 15 percent and four people per home, there may be up to approximately fourteen ultimately become *real* prospects for your church, it seems obvious that the potential is great and that a regular census is essential for the *future* of the church.

Should someone answering the door when you call want to know, "Why are you doing this?" tell him, "Approximately one out of every five families move each year, and this is our way of locating them, that we may be of service when needed."

One of the public utilities, Welcome Wagon, and a variety of other organizations can be a ready source of up-to-date information on new families moving into your community. Check and use the best one available to you. It is most important to encourage your own membership to be alert to new families.

To be worthwhile, a census, or any form of developing a prospect list for your church, requires a lay calling program to follow it up. The pastor should be interested and participate, but his time will be primarily occupied with the special situations that need his attention that emerge from lay calling and the sick and counseling calling. Therefore, a lay person should be enlisted as chairman or "head" of the calling program, and a secretary should be enlisted to help keep the records up to date and assist in scheduling calls to be made on each visitation. The chairman's function is to promote the program, to enlist additional participation, and to schedule training and inspiration events, and prospect developments, as needed. All these leadership endeavors, of course, are made in consultation with the pastor.

The first job for the secretary, in cooperation with the chairman, pastor, and church staff, is to set up the prospect record system. This is usually done with a card file. Exhibits 4-A, 4-B, and 4-C are examples of cards and types of information used by some churches. You may wish to design and have printed a card that meets your particular needs. The more complete information of Exhibit 4-C is desirable and attainable if you set it up and *determine* to keep it complete. If you are not prepared for a more disciplined program, then Exhibit 4-B is more practical. Please note especially the "objective in visiting" section of Exhibit 4-A. Like any other endeavor, a clear objective will result in more effective calling. Whatever reporting system you use, it is *important* that the date, the caller's name, and a summary of the call be recorded for the benefit of the pastor and subsequent callers.

Exhibits 4-D and 4-E are examples of forms used during a church worship period to obtain pertinent information. Exhibit 4-F is an example of a decision record form used in calling.

God's work is important and should be done in a businesslike way. Have any decisions made recorded. This is useful in impressing on the mind of the one making the decision precisely what he is doing and therefore making it more rememberable. It also serves to make sure the correct information is recorded in the church records and also passed on to the pastor for any needed follow-up. We Americans are ready to sign our names to mortgages and all types of other commitments. Experience shows that with the proper presentation and challenge, we will also make a commitment to the church. Usually the only statement necessary is something like "Our pastor will be pleased to hear about your decision. It will help us to properly record your decision in the church records and report to our pastor if you would carefully check the decision card and then sign it."

What do you say in making a call? How do you overcome objections? When and how do you persist in getting a decision when making a call? These details will not be discussed here. Others have made outstanding presentations using these techniques. Several are listed here for your preference. Some may be secured through your denominational publishing house or local bookstore. Others are obtained only by arranging for training courses for your church.

1. Tidings Publishing House has a comprehensive flipchart and/or filmstrip for use in training callers in visitation evangelism (1908 Grand Avenue, Nashville, Tennessee 37203).
2. The Coral Ridge Program for Lay Witness, D. James Kennedy, Tyndale House Publishers (Wheaton, Illinois).
3. Campus Crusade for Christ International (Arrow Head Springs, San Bernardino, California 92403).
4. Project Winsome Internationale, available only by arranging for the training course (Box 111, Bakersfield, California 93302).

Used as intended, all of these, as well as many others, can be effective in your church. All use the same basic principles. From personal experience with each of the above, our preference for starting a program is Project Winsome. The reason is simplicity. It has been reduced to the simplest language and briefest form, which makes it more readily understood, tried, and accepted by more lay people. Of great importance also is the fact that the training is designed for use within the framework of the organized church. This is not true of all programs of this type. Some fail to properly recognize the role of the organized church. It is our belief that all Christian organizations should be complementary to, rather than a fragment of, the local church.

A goal of 10 percent of the congregation as a minimum should be set to be enlisted in a calling program. From the census and other methods, a prospect list should be maintained that is as large as possible, but at least three times as large as the number of callers in your program. A sure way to kill enthusiasm for calling is to let the prospect list dwindle to just those inactive members who may have been on the list for years. This is not to suggest that the inactive not be called on. They should. It does take a more experienced caller or the pastor to handle some of these, because they have special problems.

Most importantly, make sure that you and your people understand the Biblical teaching and use Jesus' example as a basis for setting up a calling program. Experience in leading training programs for many churches who were trying to get started, or desired to improve or expand their calling program, shows the following. When the pastor and key leaders are understanding and committed to outreach, the impact of these training sessions is dramatic. When commitment is lacking, the results can be mediocre to nil. As examples, the following are quotations from pastors, received one and two years after visitation training and start of calling.

"In our case the calling program never really did get off the ground." In this case the pastor knew his church needed such a program and scheduled it. About thirty-five people participated, and for a few months it worked well and a significant number of people were brought into the church. Not one deacon of the church, however, participated. The pastor said the deacons did not see the need, but he did and wanted to go ahead. This lack of elected lay leadership ultimately caused failure, although there was initial success. It also undoubtedly caused those younger and less experienced members who tried to help the pastor to "get it off the ground" to lose confidence in the church and its system.

"You will be happy to know that we are still reaping the benefits and blessings of that November weekend. We have had decisions almost every Sunday since the project. We are thankful to God for the project, along with the impact of your personal commitment to Christ."

"It was indeed a highlight in our church year for you to be with us in a Project Winsome weekend. From that experience, we have the largest number of prospects, visits, and positive responses that I have ever seen in a church visitation project. Our church received 116 new members during the past year. Our attendance grew at both worship services. We are buying a second bus for our children's ministry. We hired an associate minister. And our budget increased by 80 percent. Your time with us certainly began a great year, and we shall always be appreciative."

"Unfortunately, when I brought my laymen together for evaluation, the men felt the program was too manipulative and unnatural. Therefore, it was laid to rest."

Many other examples could be given—both positive and negative. For the reasons previously given, and based on desire, attitude, and unity, it is almost possible to predict in advance the results of launching a visitation program. As the quotation at the beginning of this chapter says, "Virtue is the doing." If you want to succeed in anything, plan it well and do it.

Service—As Outreach

The Book of James in the Bible is built around the theme that "faith without works is dead." So if we are to show our faith by our works, what are some of the ways we can do it?

Some show their faith by being a Bible teacher or filling one of the many jobs centered within the local church building. These are good endeavors, but are not likely to offer real opportunity or appeal to the majority of the congregation.

In this section we are dealing with outreach that serves primarily the *physical and mental needs of people*, because as Christians we are commanded to love as God has loved us. These services are offered to Christian and non-Christian alike, simply because God created all, and this form of service may be the only opportunity to demonstrate God's love, gain the attention of many, and make Christian converts of many people.

Many forms of service are of such magnitude that they can only be done in cooperation with other churches. Here we are considering primarily the local congregation. Depending on the size of church, the following should be considered.

1. *Recreation.* Baseball, basketball, and team sports in general do not require large expenditures for equipment. In larger churches this can be a self-contained program or done in cooperation with community organizations and other churches. Where competitive leagues are formed, smaller churches usually pursue the latter course.

2. *Day care centers.* Nationwide, approximately 40 percent of wives work. A significant percentage of these have small children. Many of these children have a totally inadequate environment. A real opportunity to meet physical, mental, and spiritual needs exists.

Because state laws govern the operation of day care centers, these should be determined as a first order of business, so that one can know one's capability to handle and also to avoid bitter disappointment to some enthusiastic leaders and prospects. *Do not try to get by with less than is required by law.*

3. *Kindergarten or secular education.* Try only if you have a larger than average congregation fully committed to this type of ministry, and only if this sort of education very inadequately accomplished in the public realm.

4. *Nursing homes.* If a need is documented, government financing can be secured. If not operated by the church, many ministries of service to the aged are still possible. Check with a local home to determine these needs.

5. *Low-cost housing.* Although government financing is now suspended, some form is likely to return. One hundred percent financing has been possible over the last few years to any nonprofit organization documenting a good case. The key here is involving an experienced and trustworthy developer to assist in the whole project, from the market study to determine the need, to construction. Then get a real estate agent to manage under the policy of the church. Planning and conducting seminars for low-income people in how to shop, how to maintain a home and the appliances and furniture therein, and other related matters, have been found needed and successful under leadership which included those involved.

6. *Participation in local government.* The church could avoid much of the crusade image it now has and which has led to ineffectiveness if through its membership, as a policy matter, it participated in local government and helped formulate proper programs instead of starting to fight after the battle is lost.

7. *Mission.* While all we have been discussing is *mission*, the term in the average church member's mind remains one of foreign involvement—"a place that I can support with my money instead of my talent." Supporting with money is both good and essential, but here we suggest a deeper involvement. The Mormon church shows that it can be done with their two years of service to the church program. More professional people such as doctors and engineers are using vacations to give of their talents to the disadvantaged. Federal government programs such as the Peace Corps and Vista

give these opportunities to all ages. More and more business corporations are providing the opportunity for their employees to take up to one-year "leave of service to society."

We, the church, must get busy providing the spiritual depth and motivation that will make Christians want to use these opportunities to serve God by serving their fellowman.

8. *Meals on wheels.* This is community service for shut-ins who otherwise could not provide for their own care. This service is provided in many communities.

9. *Alcoholism and drugs.* The pastor, qualified lay people and local doctors can be enlisted in a formalized counseling service. People with problems in this area often do not know where to go for help. Set up and properly publicized, it will get heavy usage if a policy of privacy is maintained regarding the users of the service. The church and a pastor have a great advantage in starting such a service. With over 10,000,000 alcoholics and even more drug users in the United States the need is great in most local communities.

10. One church in Florida operates a retreat and enrichment ministry for other pastors. They have a building to house up to twenty pastors and wives and provide a program of study, relaxation, and inspiration for one week. Any group of pastors or denomination may schedule its use.

In summary, in the subject of outreach, as in every other area of ministry, we may conclude again that the secret of success is to plan well, stay within your capacity to do, and whatever you undertake do well.

EXHIBIT 4-A

 FIRST BAPTIST CHURCH, WARREN
VISITATION CARD

Area _____

Name _____ Phone _____ S.S. Class _____

Address _____ Zip _____

Children:

Church Membership: _____ Ours; _____ None; _____ Other - _____

Other Pertinent Information:

Travel Directions from Church:

Objective in Visiting
___ To win to Christ
___ To join Church
___ To enroll in Sunday School
___ To enroll children in Sunday School
___ To assist in shut-in or sickness situation
___ To enlist for leadership as: _____
___ Other:

___ To invite to attend Church
___ To become more active in Church
___ To become more active in S.S.
___ To enroll in youth program

Calling Results:

Previous Contacts:

Visitor(s) This Time _____ Date _____

Objective Achieved: _____ Yes; _____ No

Other Comments to assist in future follow-up:

95

EXHIBIT 4-B

Assignment Card for Visitation Evangelism

Name ___Burt and Carol Johnson_____

Address ___123 First Street_____

REASONS FOR BEING ON OUR RESPONSIBILITY LIST

____Member of S.S.	_____Survey—Preference	_____Attends Women's Meetings
X__Child in S.S.	__x_Member Elsewhere	_____Attends B.Y.F.
_____Child in V.C.S.	__x__Attends Church Service	_____Attends Men's Fellowship
_____Baby on Cradle Roll	____Spouse or Children	____Contributor
	Members	_____Neighborhood Contact

Other Reasons or Information_____

Called on by_____ Date_____

Report and Follow-up Recommendations_____

_____

_____

Pastor has made several calls.

Fine family. Burt (42), Carol (39).
Four children. Teenage son (Jud) in some recent difficulty.
Teenage daughter (Kit) quite interested in youth program.
Twins, Sally and Sue (8), in S.S.

Carol is a Christian but not member here.
May feel need of rededication. Attends S. S.

Burt operates successful family business.
Is searching for answers to personal needs.
Began attending services about 6 months ago.
Is open to talking about Christ. May be ready for decision.

EXHIBIT 4-C

PEOPLE SEARCH FAMILY CARD

Vacant ☐
New Construction ☐
Not at Home ☐
Refused ☐

Family Name _____ Assignment No _____

Residence Address _____ Telephone No. _____

Post Office _____ Zip Code _____ Date _____

Do not write in space	Given Name	Relation H-Husband W-Wife D-Daughter S-Son	Attendance W-Weekly M-Monthly S-Seldom N-Never		Church Member?	Where?	Local Church Preference	Date of Birth (or age)		School Grade	Chris-tian
			CH	S.S.				Month	Year		

1. How do YOU rate the family as prospects for our church? Good ☐ Possible ☐ Poor ☐

2. Remarks _____

_____

_____ 3. Canvasser _____

Code 4333-40—Broadman Supplies, Nashville, Tennessee. Printed in U.S.A.

C-Back

VISITATION REPORT

CONCERNING THE VISIT			ATTEND OUR CHURCH		CHECK SUBJECTS DISCUSSED						How do YOU rate them as prospects?	ADDITIONAL INFORMATION ABOUT FAMILY	
Dates of Visits	Home visit or telephone?	How did they respond?	Who has?	Who plans to?	Church Program	Plan of Salvation	Accepting Christ	Transfer membership	Other matters				
			N A H W C	N A H W C									
	Home Tel	Good Fair Poor									Good Poss. Poor	RESULTS OF VISIT	VISITOR

N—None, A—All, H—Husband, W—Wife, C—Children.

If the visit was by telephone, with whom did you talk? _____

97

EXHIBIT 4-D

FAITH BAPTIST CHURCH

Fort Wayne, Indiana

The Ritual of Friendship

WE WISH TO BE A FRIENDLY, FAMILY CHURCH. PLEASE JOIN US IN THE RITUAL OF FRIENDSHIP: (1) RECORD YOUR NAME, ADDRESS, AND OTHER PERTINENT INFORMATION. (2) IF YOUR ADDRESS OR PHONE NUMBER IS NEW CIRCLE IT. (3) PASS THE PAD TO THE NEXT PERSON. (4) WHEN IT REACHES THE END OF THE PEW PASS IT BACK, NOTING THE NAMES OF OTHERS. (5) AFTER THE BENEDICTION GREET OTHERS BY NAME AND INTRODUCE YOUR FAMILY.

NAME AND ADDRESS	MEMBER OF THIS CHURCH	WISH TO UNITE WITH THIS CHURCH	VISITOR	NEW RESIDENT	WISH A PASTORAL CALL	OFFERING ENVELOPES NEEDED	FOR VISITORS ONLY
Name _____ Phone ___							(I) (WE) ARE MEMBERS OF: _____ CHURCH
Address _____							IN _____ CITY _____ STATE
Name _____ Phone ___							(I) (WE) ARE MEMBERS OF: _____ CHURCH
Address _____							IN _____ CITY _____ STATE
Name _____ Phone ___							(I) (WE) ARE MEMBERS OF: _____ CHURCH
Address _____							IN _____ CITY _____ STATE
Name _____ Phone ___							(I) (WE) ARE MEMBERS OF: _____ CHURCH
Address _____							IN _____ CITY _____ STATE
Name _____ Phone ___							(I) (WE) ARE MEMBERS OF: _____ CHURCH
Address _____							IN _____ CITY _____ STATE
Name _____ Phone ___							(I) (WE) ARE MEMBERS OF: _____ CHURCH
Address _____							IN _____ CITY _____ STATE
Name _____ Phone ___							(I) (WE) ARE MEMBERS OF: _____ CHURCH
Address _____							IN _____ CITY _____ STATE

Turn to the next sheet when this one is full.

98

EXHIBIT 4-E

Welcome

To the worship and fellowship of the
Phone 662-2248 or 662-3541

FIRST BAPTIST CHURCH

Mansfield, Pennsylvania

We are asking that every person register his presence and fill-in the desired information. The ushers will receive the card at the time of the Morning Offering.

Name _____

Address _____

_____

Phone _____

[ ] I am a member of this Church.

[ ] I am a visitor today.

[ ] I am a member of the
_____ Church.

[ ] I am interested in uniting with this Church.

[ ] I wish to know more about becoming a Christian.

[ ] I am new in the community.

[ ] Desire Pastor to call in home or to visit him in the study.

[ ] Illness in family; Pastor please call.

[ ] Address has changed.

[ ] Desire set of offering envelopes.

[ ] Place my name on the Church mailing list.

[ ] Suggest call: address on other side.

Use other side for suggestions or other information.

EXHIBIT 4-F

Record of Christian Decision

----- I accept Jesus Christ as my Savior and Lord, and purpose to follow him in baptism and the Christian life, in the fellowship of his church.

----- I reaffirm my faith in Jesus Christ as my Savior and Lord, and purpose to renew my fellowship in the church by

   ----- Affirmation of faith

   ----- Transfer of letter. For my letter write to the ....

               ....Church at............................

        My name is on record there as............................

----- I will present myself to the church on............................
                                      (date)

----- I will attend a class in Christian life and church membership.

NAME............................

Address............................

(Duplicate copy may be kept by the person making the above decision)

100M 1-58 T

V

Finances

The worst education which teaches self-denial is better than the best which teaches everything else and not that.
John Sterling

A remarkably high percentage of all churches would classify themselves as "poor"—having little discretion as to what they can do, because of a lack of money—barely able to "pay the preacher." An even higher percentage fail to even begin to tap the potential income available to them.

Why? Why does this situation exist when so much attention is given to bazaars, car washes, bake sales, bingo, budgets, every member canvases, sermons, and even wishful thinking regarding an occasional rich member of a church? The answer, from our experience, is simply misdirected or insufficient effort or both. Someone once said that "he who stands for nothing, falls for everything." The church of Jesus Christ, regardless of denominational name, usually has little difficulty acknowledging belief and support of certain Christian principles, including the Bible as the Word of God to be used as the guidebook for living. But, once having agreed on the basic principles and put them in the constitution of the church, we quit. We fail to build on these principles. The easiest way to build financial support is to start with the Bible, which one should not have to sell to a membership, and teach continually its message of love, which is a message of giving. *Giving starts after the tithe has been brought into the storehouse.* A tithing church has

101

no financial problems. It is freed to spend its time in planning, setting priorities, and implementing the program that God leads it, as a people, to do. A tithing people are also likely to be much more sensitive to God's leading. A Christian has not grown very tall or mature until he has reached a height sufficient to see over the top of the pocketbook.

A significant number of churches have demonstrated the validity of this approach. The details of the strategy and implementation may vary somewhat, but generally follow this pattern.

At regular intervals there should be sermons and church school lessons on stewardship and the principle of tithing. The basic purpose *is not* for fund raising, but is part of an effort to teach the *whole* Bible. Adequate funds are a natural result, but there is a great difference if fund raising is arrived at as the purpose. The real purpose is to teach what the Bible says about tithing and giving. The natural result is twofold: (1) the blessings and joy the giver receives when accepting and following the teaching, and (2) the blessings many others receive whose lives are touched by the church programs supported by the gifts. In addition, the opportunity should be given for known tithers to share their experience and blessings from having done so. This may take a little persuading, because so many tend to "hide their light under a bushel." Telling others about being a tither is not bragging—it is sharing a Christian experience which the Bible teaches us to do. When we fail to do this, we are depriving someone else of the opportunity to grow. We are standing in the way of the progress of the Kingdom.

Next the capacity of the church as a whole to give must be determined. When this is done and communicated to all, what remains is not the question of ability to give, but the question of whether the congregation wants to give as the Bible teaches. It removes the subject from the arena of opinion—pastors, trustee, or finance committee. The following procedure has been demonstrated to be quite reliable in determining the capacity of a congregation to give money.

First, determine from the nearest IRS office the *average family income* for the *local* political subdivision in which your church is located. These numbers are usually published each year in local newspapers also. In 1973 this number is likely to be a minimum of $8,000 to $9,000 in the lowest income areas and can vary on upward to $35,000 or more in the more affluent communities. This number is higher than most pastors or lay people expect, because they forget that approximately 45 percent of all families in the United States include more than one worker. Next, determine the number of family units on your church rolls. Do not delete any because of lack of attendance—you are determining financial potential; attendance is another problem dealt with elsewhere. Multiply the *average family income* by the number of family units and you have the total income of the church family. Next, assume each family gives to the church a certain percentage of its income. Multiply this number times the total income of the church family and you have the income potential of the church at various levels of family giving. It should look something like the following:

Year	Members	Families	Average Family Income	Total Income Church Family	Church Income Potential at				
					2%	3%	4%	5%	10%
					... Thousands of Dollars ...				
1970	150	70	$8,000	$560,000	$11.2	$16.8	$22.4	$28.0	$56.0
1971	170	87	8,800	765,000	15.3	22.9	30.6	38.7	76.5
1972	200	95	9,500	902,000	18.1	27.1	36.2	45.1	90.2

The average family income figure can be checked readily by someone having a good knowledge of the people in the congregation, someone who knows the kind of job a person has, how many of a family work, etc. A reasonably knowledgeable person can go down the church roll and estimate closely what an engineer of a certain age working for a corporation is likely to be earning, and likewise a nurse, store clerk, machine tool operator, or one of any other profession. Do this, add the figures, and divide by the number of families. The average is likely to be within 1 to 3 percent of the number obtained from the IRS. If there is a difference of opinion on what the average family income should be (which is unlikely), then go through these calculations using two or three sets of income figures. From these, the people can take their choice. The potential income for the church with 10 percent giving, with any reasonable set of figures, will be so much more than presently exists in most situations that you will accomplish the objective of determining that the church has the capacity to give and now must only decide that it wants to give.

Also important to the success of this approach to financing is a unified church budget, built to support a church staff and program that has been prepared after the budget committee has given all groups or individuals who want it the chance to state their requests. A written proposed budget should then be mailed into each home with appropriate explanations one month in advance of the date on which it is to be openly discussed and adopted, or modified and adopted at a church business meeting. This budget might look like the following example.

PROPOSED BUDGET 1956

A. SALARIES		
1. Pastor	$	8000.00
2. Education Director		5600.00
3. Minister of Music		5200.00
4. Secretaries		7440.00
5. Organist		1200.00
6. Hostess		1500.00
7. Janitors		3500.00
8. Nursery Maids		1500.00
9. Kitchen Maids		700.00
10. Miscellaneous		500.00
Total		$35,140.00
B. SUNDAY SCHOOL		
1. Literature		1700.00
2. Summer Assemblies		400.00
3. Social Activities		300.00
4. Vacation Bible School		600.00
5. Promotion and Supplies		600.00
6. Study Course		150.00
7. Sunday School Clinic		200.00
Total		$ 3,950.00
C. TRAINING UNION		
1. Literature		650.00
2. Summer Assemblies		450.00
3. Social Activities		600.00
4. Training Schools		100.00
5. Promotion and Supplies		200.00
Total		$ 2,000.00
D. MISSIONARY SOCIETY		
1. GA, RA Activities		150.00
2. Summer Assemblies		100.00
Total	$	250.00

E. MUSIC DEPARTMENT	
1. Music	883.00
2. Supplies and Equipment	365.00
3. Robes	760.00
4. Summer Assemblies	350.00
5. Music Study and Activities	400.00
6. Literature	150.00
Total	$ 2,908.00
F. YOUTH ACTIVITIES	$ 800.00
G. OPERATING EXPENSE	
1. Alabama Baptist	$ 500.00
2. Auto Expense, Ed. Dir.	600.00
3. Auto Expense, Pastor	900.00
4. Auto Expense, Min. Mus.	200.00
5. Bulletin	1800.00
6. Conventions	250.00
7. Flowers	500.00
8. Insurance	2000.00
9. Janitor Supplies	500.00
10. Library	300.00
11. Office Supplies	1450.00
12. Postage	700.00
13. Publicity and Promotion	450.00
14. Revival Expense	800.00
15. Telephone	900.00
16. Utilities, Other	3600.00
17. Visual Aids	100.00
18. Maintenance, H. and G.	1250.00
19. Pulpit Supply	300.00
20. Hymnbooks	150.00
21. General Church Supplies	400.00
21. General Church Activities	500.00
23. Laundry and Dry Cleaning	200.00
24. Envelopes	750.00
25. Miscellaneous	200.00
Total	$19,300.00
H. MISSIONS	
1. Alabama Temp Alliance	120.00
2. B'ham Baptist Assoc.	720.00
3. Benevolence	500.00
4. Cooperative Program	22,486.00
5. Ministers Retirement	400.00
6. Missionary, Mrs. Moon	2000.00
7. Missionary, Miss Ryan	2000.00
8. School of Missions	300.00
9. Shades Crest Baptist Church	1800.00

10. Local Missions		250.00
11. Missionary Speakers		200.00
12. Miscellaneous		500.00
Total		$31,276.00
I. NEW BUILDINGS AND EQUIPMENT		
1. Building Fund		55,000.00
2. Office Equipment		1500.00
3. Furniture and Equipment		500.00
Total		$57,000.00
J. RESERVE 1955 BUDGET		1500.00
GRAND TOTAL		$154,124.00

The openness of this approach, with its communication of information, develops trust and unity. Almost everyone is willing to go with the majority if they have had a fair opportunity to express their views in determining the program priorities. Also, most people arrive at the same conclusion if they see the same facts—in other words, if they are informed. Also, informed people are likely to be more willing to give, because they know how their money will be used. Chapter nine will cover more on this subject as it relates to the financial program of the church.

To this point we have dealt with the procedure of education and motivation as it applies to a specific one-year program represented by a one-year budget. Two more points are important. One is that each member in some manner must personally be given the opportunity to make a decision each year as to what amount will be given in support of the Lord's work through the church. The second is a look at the long range benefits of this approach.

First, as for the personal decision to give, the most common and effective procedure to follow is an every member canvas of the members in their homes. This provides an opportunity for private discussion for those needing further understanding. The need for more information will be rare if previous procedures outlined have been done well so that canvassing can be quickly done and may amount to no more than picking up pledge cards previously mailed to the home (see chapter nine). It is most important that there are enough people to complete the canvassing in one day and that they are trained to do the job and are in complete support of the church program and procedures. Most denominations have adequate can-

106

vassing training materials; so this detail will not be covered further here.

At least one church has been most effective in the approach outlined in this chapter. They began in 1948, and the results look like this:

How we have been blessed
under one-day pledge day

1948—$ 62,000	1961—$302,000
1953—$114,000	1965—$392,000
1957—$210,000	1969—$510,818

The rain came—but so did God's people. Showers of blessings fell on us last Sunday as for the 20th consecutive year, our church pledged its entire budget in one day. Our members did not let the weather interfere, as they flocked to God's house to pledge the budget! What a testimony to the power of God! What a victory! You always respond! (Quoted from a November 1969 church bulletin)

This church, under the leadership of Dr. E. M. Arendahl, Pastor, and an effective group of lay people, well trained and organized, communicated so well that their "one-day pledge day" operation serves as an outstanding example of what can be done. Attendance on pledge day is always one of the highest, if not the highest, of any day of the year. The people enthusiastically want to be a part of this most important effort of undergirding the whole financial program of the church in one day. Having received pledge cards in the mail, most people complete them and bring to the "pledge service" held at the church school hour when everyone marches past a replica of a church building, into which the pledge cards are deposited. Those unable to attend to turn in a pledge card are quickly determined and then are called on by canvassers going out following a lunch served the canvassers immediately after the worship period. Because of the high percentage turning in pledge cards, it is unusual for any canvasser to have more than one call to make. The total of pledges turned in at the "pledge service" always exceeds the budget; so the callers have "good news" to announce to those they go to see. This also permits the caller to say, "We knew you would want to know about this and be a part of it." Receipts for the year always exceed the total pledged, even though more than 50 percent usually tithe. The success is based on a high degree of participation and tithing— not a few rich people.

It takes time to build a successful program such as this church has done. You, and your church, can do it, too—the same way Dawson Memorial did, or some modification of it—provided it is well planned and implemented on a long-range basis. Develop a good plan and stick with it.

There are many other benefits derived from the kind of financial program we advocate. The most important is spiritual growth. Let us look at some other financial benefits.

1. It permits planning each program of the church with confidence that it will meet the determined needs of the people, because you know it will be possible to finance them.

2. It permits planning church building needs for growth well in advance so that growth is not retarded by lack of space. This kind of planning and ability to finance also permits flexibility in borrowing money for construction to take advantage of the lowest possible interest rates. Over a ten- to twenty-year period, it can amount to significant money that can be used in other areas of the Lord's work.

3. It permits saving money for other uses by not having to use professional fund raisers. This is not a "knock" at these professionals; they can be useful in helping a church get started on a plan. But it seems somehow wrong for Christians to pay an outsider to fill the jobs the church members should be filling, just to ask other members for money they should be giving. As churches grow and foresee the need of additional staff, this financial system permits a careful and systematic planning for this addition—again because there will be no doubt about the ability to finance.

When it is necessary to borrow money for building or other programs, there are several ways the church can go about it:

1. local bank or savings and loan association
2. denomination sources
3. selling bonds.

Approach number one has many advantages. You will be dealing with local people, who, for a variety of reasons, have more incentive to work with and advise a local congregation. A personal acquaintance between a member of the local congregation and the local banker also may help the mutual confidence factor so important in these matters. The local bank is also likely to be more lenient in interfering with the internal affairs during those occasions of financial duress.

Use of denominational resources is most favorable in higher risk situations. Be prepared for a lot of help, some of which you may not want, but rightly so. You are the one asking for help; so be prepared with your planning and program to prove that you deserve help.

Selling bonds can be the solution under a combination of circumstances requiring *very* professional advice. A short supply of money at banks, very high interest rates, and a highly loyal congregation, willing and able to subscribe to a significant percentage of the bonds, are important considerations. B. C. Ziegler and Company, of West Bend, Wisconsin, is one company specializing in bonds for nonprofit organizations, with over fifty years experience. This is not intended as a recommendation of Ziegler, but merely a reference. Consult with your denominational headquarters and local investment banker for other references.

In the mid-1960s a Baptist church of suburban Pittsburgh, Pennsylvania, borrowed $325,000 from a bank for a building program, without any building funds in hand, without a building fund campaign, and without any key members of the church being required to sign a note or mortgage. Exhibit 5-A is the document used by the church with the bank to get a 5.5 percent interest rate loan. The bank said this was the most impressive planning they had ever seen by a church. The history and projections convinced bank officials that the church knew what it was doing and therefore was a good risk. History has proven this judgment correct and the planning of the church to be good. Had this church been required to take the time to go through a fund-raising campaign and other delays, the growth of the church would have been seriously delayed by lack of building space; and it would also have paid much higher interest rates that have prevailed most of the time since.

Remember—use finances as a tool to develop maturity and spiritual depth. Needed funds will be a natural end result.

A number of churches have made studies on the source of income in relation to the number of families recorded as givers to the church. While these studies vary somewhat in results, the following statistics are typical for a nontithing church membership:

5 percent of families give 25 to 30 percent of income
15 percent of families give 50 to 55 percent of income
50 percent of families give 95 to 100 percent of income

These same statistics reveal that 15 to 25 percent of the members fail to give through the normal envelope system; and if they contribute at all, it is in loose offerings, which represent 5 percent or less of income. Close study of this information confirms the importance of a planned, well-implemented financial effort to gain the participation of most of the people.

Another question of importance to many pastors and lay people is, Where functionally should the income be spent? How do we compare with other churches? A precise answer is not possible, because of varying conditions of size, building programs, and attitudes of people; but the following will give some reference points:

Size Church

	120 Member	750 Member	950 Member	1,800 Member
Salaries Only	31.5%	27.0%	24.0%	22.0%
Operating Expense	20.2	21.0	37.0	15.0
Building or Debt	16.3	27.0*	26.0*	35.0*
(Church School) Education (Music) (Youth)	14.0	6.0	3.0	8.0
Missions	18.0	19.0	10.0	20.0

Those churches marked by an asterisk were involved in substantial building or debt financing at the time of these budgets. The budget size varied from $40,000 for the smallest church located in an above average income community to $155,000 for the larger church in an average income community but a few years earlier in time.

As a rule of thumb, 35 percent probably is the maximum share of income that it is practical to put into a building program and remain fiscally responsible. How much should go to missions is debatable, because it is difficult to say how much of local effort is true mission. Many leaders tend to classify only that going through denominational headquarters as mission. While cooperation denominationally is a highly desirable situation, a strong local and growing church will give more through the denomination over a fifteen- to twenty-year span of time than it will give over the same period if it retards its local outreach by lack of adequate funding. In the world of the 1970s and beyond, to be effective in its ministry having a varied, appealing, and professional program, the minimum size of a local church must be larger than the majority of Protestant congregations in existence.

At what level and in what manner should a pastor be paid? This has received far too little attention in most churches. For the amount of formal education involved to be formally trained, pastors and church staff in general are grossly underpaid. These people have families to clothe, feed, and educate. As Christians, all of us are called upon to be full-time ministers. A pastor just happens to be the spiritual leader of ministers and should be paid the same salaries given to those beginners in other professions whose education skills are similar; and those salaries should be thereafter increased according to the results of the ministry performed. Performance standards should be established, the pastor should be evaluated annually against the standard.

A pastor has less opportunity to accumulate funds for future needs such as education than do most professionals. The major reason is because most churches furnish a parsonage for the home. Other professionals buy their homes and thereby have an enforced savings plan. It seems appropriate that the church should allow the pastor this same privilege—yes, even insist on it. The church then can pay a housing allowance in addition to salary and let the pastor house his family as he desires and free the congregation of being in the housing business. Some of the sample budgets in this section illustrate what some churches do—although none do enough.

In addition to base salary and housing, other costs incurred by professional staff that should be budgeted are as follows:

Travel. The average pastor travels approximately 15,000 miles per year on church business. It costs today ten to eleven cents per mile to own and operate an average size car. With energy costs going up, this will go higher also. It should be provided by the church.

Pension. Most denominational plans are reasonably competitive and should be provided.

Continuing Education. Most organizations expect professional staff to stay up-to-date in their field and/or improve their performance by broadening their background. You will have a better pastor by doing likewise. Seminars, books, and related activities are examples to be considered. Costs vary on time and travel required. From $200 to $1,000 is the right range, depending on experience, location, and need.

Hospitality. Almost every pastor has to use his home for a variety of entertaining. He must entertain church groups and other guests, such as denomination and church leaders. Make provision for this in your budget.

Memberships. If you expect your pastor to be a member of Rotary or other service clubs, then reimburse membership fees and cost of meals.

When you consider that an engineer right out of college today with a B.S. degree will be paid a minimum of $800 per month plus fringe benefits, you should have some idea of where to start when considering how to pay your pastor. It should not be the church's prerogative to discount the pastor's compensation because of his dedication to the pastorate. Let him decide what to give to the church, just as you do.

It is also evident that most churches do not spend enough in their educational ministry in relation to its importance. Whether we like it or not, the budget reflects the relative importance we attach to activities. Look at yours and see if you get any ideas as to why some of your programs fail.

EXHIBIT 5-B

BAPTIST CHURCH
COLUMBUS, MISSISSIPPI

Proposed Budget for the Year 1970

	1969 Budget	1970 Budget
I. MISSIONS		
1. Cooperative Program (20% of total budget less debt retirement)	$13,333	$16,400
2. Lowndes County Baptist Association	351	120
3. Lowndes County Baptist Camp	351	120
4. Baptist Children's Village	125	250
5. Benevolent Fund	500	750
	$14,660	$17,640
II. MUSIC		
1. Literature and Music	$ 1,350	$ 1,300
2. Piano and Organ Maintenance	350	300
3. Robes for Chapel Choir	250	250
4. Robes for Carol Choir	—	1,440
5. Mission Trip for Sanctuary Choir	—	250
	$ 1,950	$ 3,540
III. YOUTH		
1. Revival—Youth Week	$ 150	$ 200
2. Youth Retreat	200	100
3. Mission Trips (Youth)	1,800	1,000
(Youth Night Convention)	200	—
(Gulfshore Trip, Juniors)	300	—
	$ 2,650	$ 1,300
IV. EDUCATION		
1. Literature for Church Organizations	$ 3,000	$ 3,000
2. Refreshments—Banquets—Socials	1,200	1,500
3. Vacation Bible School	300	300
4. Baptist Record	375	500
5. Library	500	500
6. Baptist Bookstore (Supplies for Church	1,000	1,000
7. Miscellaneous Educational Supplies	500	500
8. Gifts for Outside Help	250	250
9. CAVE Program (Films, Audiovisual Aids)	315	315
10. Pastor's Library Expense	—	250
	$ 7,440	$ 8,115

113

	1969 Budget	1970 Budget
V. OPERATING EXPENSES		
1. Utilities: Church	$ 2,500	$ 2,750
Pastor's Home	500	600
Minister of Music's Home	500	600
2. Office Supplies	400	500
3. Postage	250	250
4. Pastor's Convention Expense	400	400
5. Minister of Music's Convention Expense	400	400
6. S. S. Supt. T. U. Dir., W.M.U. Dir., Bro. Dir., Organist, Pianist, Choir Dir., Assembly Exp.	300	350
7. Pastor's Automobile Expense	1,200	1,200
8. Minister of Music's Automobile Expense	900	900
9. Pulpit Supply	150	150
10. Annuity—Pastor and Minister of Music	800	800
11. Health and Accident Ins.—Pastor and M. M.	550	550
12. Social Security Taxes—Church's Share	1,025	1,850
13. Flowers for Church Auditorium	250	250
14. Pastor's Out-of-Town Trips	150	150
15. Minister of Music's Out-of-Town Trips	100	100
16. Revival Expenses (2)		
Evangelist	600	600
Music Director	350	400
Advertising	100	150
Lodging	200	200
17. Maintenance on Church Property	1,500	2,000
18. Furniture and Equipment (new)	1,250	1,250
19. Janitorial Supplies	850	850
20. Advertising (Church Directory Service)	15	15
21. Advertising (Radio)	100	100
22. Auditing Fee	200	200
23. Insurance on all Church Property	660	880
24. Miscellaneous Expenses	300	300
25. Planning Committee	—	400
	$16,500	$19,145
VI. SALARIES		
1. Pastor	$ 7,515	$ 8,400
2. Music—Education—Youth	7,200	8,000
3. Church Secretary	4,800	4,500
4. Organist—Youth Director	—	4,800
(Financial Secretary	1,200	—
5. Nursery Workers (3)	1,000	1,000
6. Janitor	3,400	3,400
7. Pianist	960	960
	$26,075	$31,060

VII. DEBT RETIREMENT FUND	$13,440	$13,440
VIII. BUILDING FUND	1,200	1,200
TOTAL BUDGET	$83,915	$95,440

EXHIBIT 5-C

BAPTIST CHURCH

Treasurer's Report—1968

	1968 Budget	Expenditures	Over (+) Under (—)
A. SALARIES			
1. Pastor	$ 8600.00	$ 8600.00	$ —
2. Assistant Pastor	4500.00	—	4500.00 —
3. Secretary	4500.00	4495.38	4.62 —
4. Music Director	825.00	723.75	101.25 —
5. Organist	1300.00	1345.00	45.00 +
6. Custodian	4300.00	4266.92	3.08 —
7. Pulpit Supply	300.00	255.00	45.00 —
8. Reserve and Revival	500.00	336.80	163.20 —
9. Social Security	350.00	392.12	42.12 +
TOTAL A	$25175.00	$20414.97	$ 4760.03 —
B. SUNDAY SCHOOL			
1. Literature	$ 1800.00	$ 1585.92	$ 214.08 —
2. Supplies and Promotion	700.00	259.47	440.53 —
3. Study Courses and Clinic	100.00	—	100.00 —
4. Vacation Bible School Under (—)	250.00	184.43	65.17 —
5. Mission School	200.00	213.08	13.08 +
6. Summer Camps	100.00	32.50	67.50 —
7. Miscellaneous	150.00	89.87	60.13 —
8. Library	250.00	38.56	211.44 —
TOTAL B	$ 3550.00	$ 2403.83	$ 1146.17 —
C. TRAINING UNION			
1. Literature	$ 250.00	$ 174.72	$ 75.28 —
2. Supplies and Promotion	100.00	82.83	17.17 —
3. Social Activities	250.00	164.57	85.43 —
4. B. Y. F. Convention	100.00	100.00	—
TOTAL C	$ 700.00	$ 522.12	$ 177.88 —
D. MISSION SOCIETY			
1. Literature, Program Material	$ 70.00	$ 27.93	$ 42.07 —

2. Women's Conference of W. Pa.	60.00	60.00	—
3. White Cross	85.00	160.73	75.73 +
4. State Scholarship Fund	15.00	15.00	—
5. State Refit Fund	15.00	15.00	—
6. Association Contribution	25.00	25.00	——
7. United Church Women of So. Sub.	15.00	15.00	—
8. Christmas Gifts—R. C. C. and B. H.	20.00	30.00	—
9. Christmas Gifts—Spec. Int. Miss.	20.00	20.00	—
10. Rankin Spring Project	15.00	15.00	—
11. Southwestern Baptist Camp	20.00	20.00	—
12. Mather School	180.00	180.00	—
13. Haiti Scholarship	240.00	240.00	—
14. Christian Service Projects	85.00	24.20	60.80 —
15. Annual Baptist Homes Party	40.00	20.31	19.69 —
16. Annual Tea—Rankin Chr. Center	5.00	5.00	—
17. 3 Sub. to Amer. Bap. Woman	3.75	—	3.75 —
18. Pioneer Girls	25.00	25.00	—
19. Christian Service Brigade	25.00	25.00	—
20. Miscellaneous	35.00	120.29	85.29 +
TOTAL D	$ 1008.75	$ 1043.46	$ 34.71 +

E. MISSION GIFTS

1. ABC World Mission Support	$12000.00	$12000.00	$ —
2. Love Gifts	As given	See below	—
3. Baptist Homes	1000.00	1000.00	—
4. American Bible Society	100.00	100.00	—
5. Minimum Salary Plan—P.B.C.	100.00	100.00	—
6. Ministers' and Missionaries' Fund	100.00	100.00	—
7. Pittsburgh Baptist Association	200.00	202.50	2.50 +
8. Benevolences (Deacons' Fund)	750.00	221.75	528.25 —
9. Southwestern Baptist Camp	600.00	600.00	—
10. World Fellowship Offering	300.00	300.00	—
11. America for Christ Offering	300.00	300.00	—
12. Rankin Christian Center	200.00	200.00	—
13. Eastern Baptist Seminary	100.00	100.00	—
14. Pioneer Girls	100.00	100.00	—
15. Christian Service Brigade	100.00	100.00	—
16. James and Nancy Harris	500.00	500.00	—
17. Miscellaneous	100.00	—	$ 100.00
TOTAL E	$16550.00	$15924.25	$ 625.75 —

F. YOUTH ACTIVITY

1. General	$ 100.00	$ 77.42	$ 22.58 —
2. Retreats	200.00	15.00	185.00 —

117

			Over (+)
3. Athletics	500.00	689.65	189.65 +
4. Guild	100.00	29.65	70.35 —
TOTAL F	900.00	$ 811.72	$ 88.28 —

	1968 Budget	Expenditures	Over (+) Under (—)
G. MUSIC DEPARTMENT			
1. Robes	$ 300.00	$ 52.57	$ 247.43 —
2. Music	300.00	308.57	8.57 +
3. Miscellaneous	200.00	24.60	175.40 —
TOTAL G	$ 800.00	$ 385.74	$ 414.26 —
H. OPERATING EXPENSE			
1. Crusader & Missions Magazine	$ 350.00	$ 306.00	$ 44.00 —
2. Bulletins	300.00	331.14	31.14 +
3. Pastors' Auto Allowance	1500.00	1000.00	500.00 —
4. Conventions	250.00	33.00	217.00 —
5. Decorations and Flowers	300.00	264.02	35.98 · —
6. Insurance	1300.00	1460.92	160.92 +
7. Taxes	500.00	557.29	57.29 +
8. Utilities	2700.00	3189.46	489.46 +
9. Maintenance	3000.00	2123.65	876.35 —
10. Janitor Supplies	400.00	313.31	86.69 —
11. Office Supplies	500.00	444.83	55.17 —
12. Postage	500.00	717.25	217.25 +
13. Envelopes	200.00	146.02	53.98 —
14. Publicity	350.00	293.51	56.49 —
15. Social Activities	150.00	861.48	711.48 +
16. Ministers' and Missionaries' Fund	2625.00	1714.50	910.50 —
17. Miscellaneous	1000.00	876.94	123.06 —
18. Housing Allowance (Pastor)	2500.00	2500.00	—
19. Utilities (Parsonage)	425.00	—	425.00 —
20. Child Care	1200.00	121.25	1078.75 —
TOTAL H	$20050.00	$17254.57	$ 2795.43 —
J. BUILDING AND EQUIPMENT			
1. Mortgage Payments	$27000.00	$26832.00	$ 168.00 —
TOTAL J	$27000.00	$26832.00	$ 168.00 —

118

K. FURNITURE AND FIXTURES

	1968 Budget	Expenditures	Over (+) Under (—)
1. Office Equipment	$ 500.00	$ —	$ 500.00 —
2. Chairs and Tables	$ 500.00	$ —	$ 500.00 —
TOTAL K	$ 1000.00	$ —	$ 1000.00 —

	1968 Budget	Expenditures	Over (+) Under (—)
L. CONTINGENT FUND	$ 1000.00	$ 686.06	$ 313.94 —
GRAND TOTAL	$97733.75	$86279.72	$11454.03 —
LOVE GIFTS (E-2)		$ 2543.14	
TOTAL EXPENDITURES		$88822.86	

1968	Income	Expenditures
January	$ 5757.89	$ 6383.18
February	6200.86	5955.25
March	8171.07	7551.54
April	7283.43	8247.29
May	9388.35	9216.31
June	8503.55	7362.26
July	6678.67	7360.47
August	6300.31	6933.87
September	8370.88	6126.33
October	6722.90	8299.61
November	8093.76	6649.87
December	17472.68	8736.88
TOTAL	$98944.05	$88822.86

Balance January 1, 1968	$ 821.40
Income, 1968	98944.05
Check #6586—Outdated	10.00
Check #6637—Error	10.00
Check #6658—Void	30.00
Check #6843—Void	20.00
	$99835.45
Check #6925—Error	.20
	$99835.25
Expenditures, 1968	88822.86
Balance, January 1, 1969	$11012.39

119

Savings Account—#X3994		Savings Account—#1777	
Pews	$ 8150.44	Scholarship Fund	$ 1378.74
Building Fund	1899.07		
Communion Chairs	57.25		
Memorial—Rev. A. F. Ballbach	20.00		
Opportunity Day	1678.19	Mortgage Balance	
Savings Account	1042.50	January 1, 1969	$308,585.28
	$12847.45		

EXHIBIT 5-D

1974 PROGRAM PROPOSAL

Anticipated Expenditures

Pastoral Ministry		
Salary	8,900	
Car Allowance	1,500	
Utilities	840	
Pension and Hospitalization	2,350	
Convention Expense	250	13,840
CHRISTIAN EDUCATION—Al Knerler		
Curriculum Materials, Supplies and Equipment	900	
Camps, Conferences, and Vacation Bible School	150	1,050
WORSHIP—Don DeCecco		
Organist and Choir Director	650	
Supplies and Maintenance	200	
Communion and Worship Supplies	50	
Pulpit Supply (Guest Preachers)	250	
	250	1,150
OFFICE—Sally Lightholder		
Secretary	2,340	
Mimeograph Supplies	200	
Printing	200	
Postage	300	
Telephone	350	3,390
PROPERTY MAINTENANCE—Scott VanHoose		
Janitor	2,400	
Utilities	1,400	
Church and Education Buildings and Grounds	700	
Parsonage and Yard	250	
Insurance and Taxes	1,112	5,862
DEBT SERVICE		
Church and Education Buildings (ABEC)	6,500	
Parsonage (Mt. Lebanon S. and L.)	3,332	
New Lot (ABEC)	972	10,804
BENEVOLENCE—Kathleen Wheeley		
American Baptist World Mission (Undesignated)	2,300	

121

American Baptist Related Institutions:
    Pittsburgh Baptist Association (Dues)   100
    Rankin Christian Center   200
    The Baptist Home   200
    Laurel Highlands Baptist Camp   50

BENEVOLENCE
    American Baptist Related Institutions:
    Bacone College   200
    Alderson-Broaddus College   200
    Ellen Cushing Jr. College   100
    Eastern Baptist College   100
    Eastern Baptist Seminary   100
    Andover Newton Theological School   100
    Other Concerns:
    South Hills Interfaith Ministry   200
    American Bible Society   50
    American Leprosy Mission   50
    Contingency   150   4,100

    40,196

VI

Education

A man's mind may be likened to a garden, which may be intelligently cultivated or allowed to run wild; but whether cultivated or neglected, it must, and will bring forth. If no useful seeds are put into it, then an abundance of weed seeds will fill therein, and will continue to produce their kind.

Allen

In this chapter the primary subject will be the church school and Bible study. The educational process should go much further, however; so also to receive attention will be education in church membership, and the many job functions filled by lay people.

Scientists, businessmen, government leaders and people from all walks of life have testified to their faith in a Supreme Being and the great value in Christian education.

The late, world-famous J. C. Penney often stated, "All I am today I owe to my religious training as a boy. Of course, much of this came from my parents, but a good deal of it came through the Sunday schools which I attended."

Carl W. Miller, a scientist, stated, "Can any thoughtful person doubt that the cultivation of religion and the sense of moral responsibility inevitably associated with it are prime requisites for a people that would be master of its own destiny? Let this aspect of general education lapse, and our prized democracy can no longer survive."

Judge L. L. Fawcett of Brooklyn, New York, has been quoted; "I have been on the bench for twenty-three years and over 4,000 boys and girls have been brought before me for varying degrees of misconduct, and only three of these have been regular in Sunday school attendance. Fathers and mothers, my advice to you is to take your boys and girls and go to Sunday school."

William Allen White phrased it well: "The child who does not go to Sunday school, who has no knowledge of the source out of which our civilization sprung, who is ignorant of the vast literature called the Bible . . . is not ready to do his part in our American democracy. He starts handicapped . . . the Sunday school is the best preparation for peace and stability that the world can make."

With such strong evidence in support of it, why has church school attendance gone steadily down and become much lower than the 40 percent of the United States population that attends church? Why have some churches dropped it completely and many others stopped Bible study for adults?

There are many reasons to be discussed, along with suggestions as to what to do about it. But first, a generalization comes from many years of service, both as a teacher and as a Sunday school superintendent. The vast majority of people, including regular attendees, do not really understand the purpose of the whole process. Bible study is thought of in terms of quoting scriptural verses and gaining knowledge (both are all right) instead of spiritual development.

The basic purpose of Bible study is to develop a sensitivity to God—a sensitivity that permits an individual in daily life to distinguish between God's leading and his own desires or those of others. *Regular* Bible study, worship, prayer, and service are essential in accomplishing this sensitivity; but Bible study is the foundation.

Infrequent Bible reading may make a momentary "visible" impression, but rarely is it lasting. Regular Bible study along with worship, on the other hand, impresses itself upon the mind and soul of a person in a manner that develops a high degree of sensitivity to God. This should be the objective of every church school, teacher, and student. It is the relationship to God that is important; knowledge, faithfulness and many other valuable side benefits will also result.

How can you accomplish this objective with a Christian education program in your church?

First, there must be a common understanding among all the church leadership that the objective is desirable and a will to do that which is necessary to accomplish it. This is essential, because every leader, regardless of position, will either contribute toward or detract from reaching the objective. If you do not believe it, take a Tinker-toy set and dump it out onto a table before your leaders and ask them to build something. You will quickly see either a study in frustration and failure or agreement on an objective—what to build.

Dr. John A. Lavender, pastor of the First Baptist Church of Bakersfield, California, likes to simplify the goals of a church school as follows:

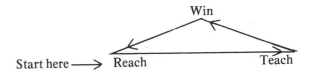

There must be an outreach to bring people in. People are brought in that the Bible may be taught. The Bible is taught that God may win them to a faith in and commitment to Him through Jesus Christ. Then the cycle repeats. The person won continues study in order to grow so that God, through that person, may reach others to be taught or served in some other Christian way.

Accomplishing this cycle requires (1) an organization, (2) a trained teaching staff, (3) a graded Bible curriculum, (4) a reasonably comfortable meeting room, and (b) a requirement of accomplishment of the pupils. Without these five, the following important learning tasks are not likely to be accomplished:

Listening
Exploring
Discovering
Appropriating
Assuming responsibility.

Organization

Regardless of the style of organization you may have in your church (see chapter two), someone must be in charge of the church school. It cannot be effectively run by a board or committee. Elect a church school superintendent or a Christian education director and give him full responsibility for administering the education program within the broad policy guidelines established by the congregation or governing board. The following are typical policies:

1. It is the policy of the church to use the Christian education curriculum published by the denomination with which the church is affiliated.
2. The church school will consist of a minimum of fifty-two one-hour sessions meeting each Sunday at 9:45 A.M.
3. The church school superintendent will be elected annually by the congregation and may not serve more than five consecutive terms.
4. Every other officer and teacher of the school will be appointed by the superintendent for a one-year term.
5. A record system shall be maintained, suitable for measuring the efficiency and effectiveness of the school.

There could be other policies required for specific circumstances, but they should be kept to a minimum. Beyond policy making in broad terms, the board's function should be restricted to one of an advisory and evaluative service to the superintendent—never one of supervision.

The remainder of the organization might look like the chart on the following page. This chart represents a suitable structure for church schools of 300 to 500 members. In smaller schools, some consolidation may be necessary, such as eliminating the Middler Department by combining the third grade with primary and the fourth grade with the junior department. In larger schools, more classes could be created per department, and possibly more adult departments, when the size is above 100 students.

126

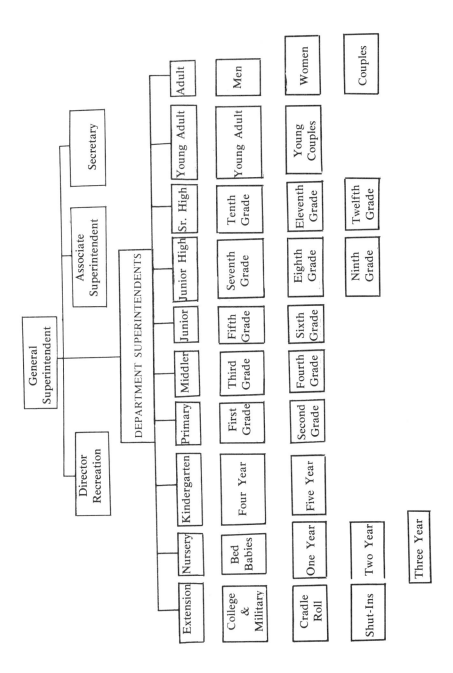

127

Since this organization is essentially graded by age (school ages are graded by public school class), we should discuss the reasons for grading before going on to the administrative and teaching functions.

Some say you cannot make grading work in the world of the 1970s. A few say it is undemocratic, that you must let each individual decide into which class he wants to go. These statements show a lack of understanding, communication, or desire. Grading works when understood. Most people can see the advantages, some of which are outlined below.

Church schools did not invent grading by age. At birth we are all graded, because we arrive at different times. This difference continues throughout life. When we follow this grading system in the church school, we are merely working in harmony with the laws of God. Age (or public school class) grading automatically fixes responsibility for the unenlisted. An unenlisted seventh grader is assigned to the seventh grade class—just as a forty-two-year-old would be assigned to the class whose age span included 42. It prevents the classes with the best leadership from getting too large at the expense of others. It insures an exchange between different social, economic, and cultural levels. This enhances the climate for spiritual growth. Although anyone can find exceptions, experience in many schools shows this system also generally brings these additional benefits:

1. People of similar needs are brought together.
2. Faster and more stable growth of the person and the school occurs.
3. It is easier to form new classes to accommodate growth.
4. It creates a better teacher-learning situation.
5. It creates a better environment for class participation.
6. It underscores the importance of the individual.

If a prospect who visits a class is to become a member and to be retained, the class must be friendly and the teaching effective. If teaching is effective, friendliness will be present. The teacher must involve those present in Bible study which leads to discovery of truths and which, in turn, will change lives when practiced. A member whose spiritual needs are being met is not likely to be a dropout, and a prospect who sees in the class the possibility of regular, spiritually satisfying learning can be enrolled.

While there are social and other benefits to be derived from the church school, Bible study and spiritual development are the only things that you can be reasonably sure of doing better than can be done elsewhere. Stray too far from this basic purpose and success will be elusive.

The teacher should teach and lead by example all class members to be concerned about the needs of unenrolled or erratic attendees for the Lord and for regular Bible study. Names and addresses of prospects are necessary and are usually available when the outreach methods discussed in another chapter are practiced by the church. Others should be discovered by class members among their neighbors, friends, and fellow workers. Give responsibility to a class member for a prospect. Encourage the member to cultivate the prospect through regular contact, which may include home visitation, recreational activities, lunch, or class social functions. Cultivation is important whether the person is enrolled or not, and should include ministry in time of need, happy occasions, and the personal expression of one's faith.

Classes should be relatively small in size (children—ten to fifteen enrolled; youths—fifteen to twenty enrolled; adults—twenty-five to thirty enrolled). Classes on the low side of these ranges have room to grow. Small classes stimulate members to enlist others. An assigned age range enables a class to concentrate on a group for whom it alone is responsible. A class should be organized with a president, vice president, and secretary. In addition to the leadership training received by being an officer, the officers should take the lead in helping the teacher set the example in visitation and cultivation, to ensure growth. The purpose of growth should not be just an increase in numbers, but an attempt to show that a human being is created, loved by God, and that God loves and wants us to love.

How do you recognize a good Bible class or church school? Or, to put it another way, what are some targets that will insure good results if they are achieved? American Baptist Churches for many years used the following:

The great objective of Christian education is the new person in Jesus Christ. How to guide and develop these new persons to become effective disciples of Christ is one of the aims of the Sunday Church School. In order to help the church in its job, the division of Christian Education of the Board of Education and Publication, through extensive research and study, has set up the Standard of Achievement for Baptist Sunday Church Schools. The Standard is a set of twelve fundamentals which are essential for good Christian education in any church. It can be described as a scale for measuring progress and efficiency, as a working program for an effective and growing Sunday Church School. Experience has proven that churches making use of the Standard have shown remarkable progress.

Experience even in 1974 confirms the above statement. The Standard is quoted as follows:

American Baptist Standard of Achievement
For Sunday Church Schools

I. Attendance Increase
   A. Average attendance increased at least 5 per cent
   B. The use of a definite plan for the enrollment and conservation of members
II. Leadership Training
   A. A training program in which 25 per cent of the teachers, department superintendents, and general officers earn one or more leadership education credits
   B. A minimum of six workers' conferences attended by 60 per cent of the teachers and officers
III. Church Loyalty
   A. An average of at least 60 per cent of those in attendance above the Primary Department participating in the church's program of Sunday morning worship
   B. Giving to local expenses and to the Unified Budget of the American Baptist World Mission encouraged through the use of an envelope system in all departments above the Nursery, or through a proportionate share of the weekly offering
IV. Bible Study
   A. The Bible used as the basis for study and worship in every department and class
   B. The message of the Bible taught through the use of American Baptist teaching materials in every department and class

V. World Mission

A missionary education program presenting the American Baptist World Mission through two of the following:

A. Interpretation of three areas of our denominational program in all groups above the Kindergarten

B. A missionary education library with current books in each department above Kindergarten, and a plan in operation for their use

C. Active participation in a graded church school of missions

VI. Community Witness

A. A definite plan of visitation to enroll the unreached

B. Completion of one or more projects in Christian social relations

VII. Decisions for Christ

A genuine concern to win all persons to Jesus Christ through:

A. Training teachers to interview and guide their pupils toward a decision for Christ as Lord and Savior

B. Special age-group classes in discipleship and church membership

VIII. Spiritual Enrichment

A. A program to encourage personal and family devotional practices

B. A program for the spiritual growth of teachers and officers

IX. Church-Home Co-operation

Cooperation with the home in the Christian guidance of pupils in two of the following:

A. Every pupil visited in his home by his teacher

B. The use of American Baptist materials for the home

C. Two or more parent-teacher meetings for cooperative planning

X. Effective Organization

A. The Sunday Church School related to the church through a church-related Board of Christian Education

B. The American Baptist plan of grouping and grading

XI. Summer Activities

A program which includes two of the following:

A. Summer training opportunities

B. Church school members encouraged to take advantage of opportunities in church camping

C. Active participation in a vacation church school

XII. Better Equipment

A. Evaluation of rooms and equipment in relation to pupil needs

and formulation of plans for improvement
B. Definite evidence of some improvement each year

These twelve points can be varied to accommodate any denominational considerations. It is the thought process and the implementation of the principles that is important. They work if *you* work to carry them out.

Now let us look at the administration of the school through the organization previously discussed and these twelve standards.

I. *Attendance Increase*

It is a rare church that cannot grow more than 5 percent each year, following these principles and the plan for enrollment and conservation of members discussed previously in this chapter and the chapter on outreach. The target, whether 5 percent or more for the whole school, should be specifically assigned to individual classes according to known facts. For example, the target may be one new member for a junior class, but two for an adult class of a certain age span. Make the target specific and real. Communicate it in writing and promote it regularly. Refer to the sample letter (Exhibit 6-A) at the end of this chapter.

II. *Leadership Training*

This cannot be overemphasized. Every successful organization must provide continuing education for its leaders for their enrichment and motivation. For church school workers, this can be in many forms—in-depth Bible study, teaching methods, human relations, etc. It should include attending sessions with others as well as material for personal study. It may be done in the local church, or as an association of churches, or in a college. The target of 25 percent is the minimum each year. Every teacher should be required to meet this objective at least once every four years.

Workers' conferences really should be held once per month for twelve months. These are for the purpose of training and communications. It is a great opportunity to use one worker to demonstrate a proficiency to others (See sample agenda, exhibit 6-B). When a worker has this opportunity, the preparation required to do well before fellow workers at the conference causes this person to become even better. It means actively encourage support of the whole program, with particular emphasis on worship and giving. It should be understood

Policy and procedural matters illustrated by Exhibits 6-D, 6-E, 6-F, 6-G, and 6-H are other suitable topics for workers' conference discussions. These matters should also be confirmed in writing to each worker.

One thing that a workers' conference should *not* be is a decision-making committee. All of us have experienced much loss of valuable time and manpower when the workers' conference has turned into a business session in which the workers end by trying to decide such things as who is going to bring the potato salad to the next picnic. This should be assigned for handling by someone or a committee at another time of their own choosing. Exhibit 6-I contains additional ideas.

III. *Church Loyalty*

The church school should never be permitted to become an entity unto itself. It is a part of a larger total church program, and to accomplish its purpose as previously stated, it must actively encourage support of the whole program, with particular emphasis on worship and giving. It should be understood by each worker that such support is required of the worker. Certainly a teacher who does not regularly attend the church's worship program or is not a systematic giver to the church is not able to effectively persuade others to do so. One church that has been observed closely required an elected leader to be not merely a systematic giver, but a tither. We discovered this to be a great way to challenge loyalty and commitment. Perhaps we should ask ourselves, "Isn't it about time that we quit playing church?"

IV. *Bible Study*

As a result of extensive travel and speaking engagements in churches, the author has had the opportunity to observe hundreds of church schools of several denominations in action. The variations within denominations are as great or greater than between denominations.

In some classes, one would never guess that the Bible or its application to daily living was the topic of study, because it was not. In others, the fear of contamination is so great that no outside resource material is used and the same uninspired and often uninformed effort is repeated each Sunday without success. In others, it is left up to the individual teacher to select the "literature" to use! The Bible is and should be emphasized as the text. Literature, teaching aids, and the like are supplemental materials whose purpose is to help plan a course of study that will cover the whole Bible and bring at least one other viewpoint into discussion to stimulate thought and understanding. Once a church policy is adopted as to which literature is to be used, then all classes should use it. It is preferable to use literature that has been prepared by one's own denomination. If it is not what you believe it should be, then work to get it changed. Certainly, the confusion of using anybody's and everyone's is not a suitable substitute.

The superintendent should have a group of approved teachers available to substitute when a regular teacher is sick or otherwise cannot be present. These substitutes should be encouraged to participate in workers' conferences and other activities that keep them informed and qualified to carry on in harmony with the church school objectives.

V. *World Mission*

This is a significant item in the vast majority of church budgets. Yet, experience indicates that relatively few members of most churches really know much about what is going on through their denomination's mission effort. There is considerable quiet grumbling, but not too much openly, because tradition has established missions as an untouchable budget item. Working on the principle that an informed membership will support those things about which it is informed emphasizes the need for a special effort to educate people regarding missions. This is one of the areas of the expanded concept of Christian education within the church.

VI. *Community Witness*

This point is discussed rather completely in the chapter on outreach.

VII. *Decisions for Christ*

Have you tried to find out how many of your teachers really

know how to get people to make a decision for Christ? Experience suggests, only a small percentage. No teacher can do well something for which he has no training. Training is a must, and the Christian education director or leadership should take the initiative in planning a Project Winsome or a similar program, discussed in the chapter on outreach.

Classes in discipleship and church membership are usually taught by the pastor or by a particularly experienced layman. They should be designed to inform the new member or prospective new member on the plan of salvation, ordinances observed, such as Baptism and Communion, church boards, organization, and policies. In other words, they should give a person a chance to be an informed member, so that he will want to participate before either losing interest or serving a ten-year apprenticeship. This is an important phase of Christian education, one that is totally missed in many churches.

VIII. *Spiritual Enrichment*

Some spiritual enrichment is achieved in leadership training and workers' conferences. We could further emphasize it by doing the following:

A. Bring in an outside teacher-speaker for what may be called a spiritual enrichment conference and would probably cover one and one-half hours for three to five nights.

B. Build a reference library of books and films for the church and encourage its use.

C. Encourage teachers to build their own reference library. Our experience shows that, having this encouragement at an early age, we acquire rather extensive help in this area and continue to build on it.

D. Communicate in writing once each month some thought-provoking material that motivates self-evaluation and action. Chapter nine on Promotion provides several exhibits.

If, as the Bible teaches, man's eternal good and short term wisdom comes from God and is gained through the development of the spiritual aspect of man, then spiritual enrichment is not only an appropriate objective for each church member, but is doubly important for those in leadership positions. The emphasis here is placed on the smaller leadership group, because if they get it, you will be sure that those they lead will get it also.

IX. *Church-Home Cooperation*

Although this may not appear to need elaboration, it should be emphasized that such cooperation applies to all ages, not just to youth or children. It is an area in which workers with children can be a major influence in helping to enlist parents.

X. *Effective Organization*

Comment already has been made in this chapter and the chapter on organization.

XI. *Summer Activities*

Vacation church school is an important activity that should come under the direction of the church school organization. It should be planned with two purposes in mind:

A. It is an opportunity to increase the church's teaching ministry by 50 percent to 100 percent depending on whether it is a half-day program for one or two weeks or the equivalent. At best, with perfect attendance, the regular church school program gives fifty-two hours of classroom study plus some extra study, hopefully at home. Just four hours per day for a week, because of the added benefit of concentration, probably gives a 50 percent increase in learning. For those children enlisted who have not been attending, vacation church school obviously is even more important and may mean a total change in their lives here and throughout eternity.

B. The second purpose is to enlist new members for Bible study. Unfortunately, there are parents who will enroll their children just to be able to have that "free" time for themselves and their own desires. As unfortunate as this reason may be, it nevertheless creates opportunity for the church school.

There are many denominational programs published for church vacation schools; you are referred to these for details. Suffice it to say here—keep it Bible centered, plan it well, and make it exciting. In chapter eight, we will discuss other activities.

XII. *Better Equipment*

Equipment is often overlooked but very important to evaluate each year. Room size, appearance, and comfort, related to class or department, should be considered. Unless this is done and unless changes are made on occasion, sometimes teachers become possessive and begin to think of a room as "mine." Too much of this freezes things, so that later on, needed changes may become nearly impossible. Equipment such as chairs, tables, podiums, storage facilities, lighting, and ventilation systems need to be considered. Visual aid equipment, such as projectors, blackboards, and toys, also falls into this category.

Good playthings should have the following characteristics:

1. As free of detail as possible
2. Versatile in use
3. Involve the child in the play
4. Large, easily manipulated
5. Warm and pleasant to touch
6. Durable
7. Work as intended
8. Construction easily comprehended
9. Sufficient quantity and roominess
10. Encourage cooperative play
11. Price based on durability and design.

Church School

We should now refer back to the church school organization chart, and look at the Church Extension Department. This is important for two major reasons. First, there is a need and opportunity for service. Second, unless contact is maintained through enforced absences, these become the basis for dropouts. This activity is of prime importance, and everyone on this department's roll should be contacted a minimum of once per month, and more in many instances.

The cradle roll, of course, is for newborn babies. Enroll them at this age of "beginning" and show interest and help to the mother at this time of need and you also help adult work. An appropriate memento should be given to the child.

There are shut-ins of all ages, due to illness or age. Ministry for these people then should be tailored to the need. There are many possible ways to help—shopping, meals, reading, economic assistance. College and military personnel, of course, are away for extended periods of time. Newsletters, church bulletins, birthday remembrances, and the like are excellent ways of maintaining contact that is deeply appreciated and is likely to cause a return to church upon a return home.

While teacher selection and training is important for all groups, a special emphasis is placed on three—nursery school children, senior high school students, and young adults just out of school. Nursery school is important, because this is the first impression a person gets of church school. If the impression is good, then an interest and desire is developed that may be lasting. Classes for senior high students and young adults are important in order to bridge the gap between childhood and adulthood, which is necessary for the long term survival of the church. Break the line here and there is no input to the future.

Recordkeeping

Recordkeeping is absolutely necessary for the measurement of effectiveness and quality. The system developed and used by Southern Baptist has much merit and is illustrated and discussed here. (See Exhibit 6-L, Department Report, and Exhibit 6-M, Individual Student Report.)

Notice the effort to put emphasis on quality by recording performance in studying prior to class, attendance, and punctuality. Stewardship is promoted by emphasis on giving to the church. Outreach is promoted through emphasis on visitors and new members. Obviously these things must be understood and used if they are to be of value. Experience teaches that it is a good system and requires very little effort if individual record slips are filled out by each member and turned in to the class secretary for recording.

Exhibit 6-J gives one example of a job specification for a

138

professional minister of education. There is no magic point in time to employ this professional. It depends on the economic level of the membership and their commitment to the support of the church. A professional brings special training and many more man-hours to the job. The man-hours should not be used to do all of the work, but to better plan, train, and effectively utilize the lay people so that more can be accomplished in Christian education.

A church membership between 400 and 600 can justify a second (pastor is first) full-time professional staff member. Whether it should be in education, music, or another area depends on the need—the need of the constituents, as well as the inability of the lay leadership and pastor to fill the needs.

Music is also an essential element of Christian education, but it is normally treated separately in most churches (see Exhibit 6-K). A graded choir program is a most important function of the music ministry and Christian education. If a child is started at age five or six in a church music program, a basic understanding of music is obtained by the child through growth, as well as the joy of participation and the discipline learned from group singing. Spiritual depth is also developed. How often have you seen an unhappy person singing? More comments on music will appear in the chapter on worship.

One last thought on Christian education. How many teachers ever really try to do any testing to find out where their students are in their understanding? In the days of the Greek Academy, a tutor asked his students certain questions to ascertain his level of understanding. Inability to answer a question did not mean failure; it only meant there was more work to be done to attain a genuine mastery of the subject. It was the tutor's job to determine what the nature of that work should be.

It is rare to find this understanding even in the public school or in the higher education system. Think about it. Do we really want to have success in Christian education? Or are we just playacting?

EXHIBIT 6-A

December 31, 1963

TO: Mr. John Sherwin
SUBJECT: Review of Sunday School Class Records,
             October through December

A review of attendance indicates the following individuals have either not attended at all during the fall quarter or very infrequently:

> Ray Smith
> Edward Jones
> Barbara Coleman
> Pauline Wilson
> Terry Brown

A visit in the home and contacts by other class members are suggested in order to enlist the interest and attendance of these. After a personal visit in the home, if there are those that we should remove from our rolls, please discuss with your Departmental Superintendent.

It is also suggested that you review your class record book to see whether it is being kept completely up to date and to note those points of indicated deficiency in which the students need to be encouraged to participate.

Thanks very much for your efforts, and please let me know if either I or your Departmental Superintendent can be of assistance.

Superintendent

EXHIBIT 6-B

Workers' Conference Agenda

"WHAT ARE YOU DRIVING AT?"

August 8, 1961

A. "Stronger Than Yourself" .... 5 Min.
B. Filmstrip—"S. S. Organization" #1 .... 15 Min.
C. "Why Organize?" .... 12 Min.
D. Filmstrip—"Planning the Program" #3 .... 15 Min.
E. "Problems and How to Solve Them" .... 12 Min.
F. Filmstrip—"Expansion" #4 .... 15 Min.
G. "Why Visitation" .... 12 Min.
H. Filmstrip—"No Vacant Chairs" .... 15 Min.

1 Hr. 41 Min.

EXHIBIT 6-C

<u>Workers' Conference Agenda</u>

September 8, 1961

Dear Teacher and Officer:

The September meeting will be held at the church this Tuesday evening, September 12th, between 7:45 P.M. and 9:15 P.M. The attendance was excellent at the August meeting. We especially invite those who have not been attending to come and share with us as we strive to better serve our Lord through our Christian Education program.

The program will be as follows:

Devotional .... 5 minutes
Review of past year's performance .... 20 minutes
Plans for Promotion Day and
    coming year .... 20 minutes
"The Teacher at Work" .... 45 minutes
    (a) Jesus The Great Teacher
    (b) The Teacher's Task
    (c) The Teacher's Motive
    (d) The Teacher's Relationship to the Church
    (e) The Teacher's Responsibility to Sunday School
    (f) The Teacher's Preparation
    (g) The Teacher in the Classroom

Yours in His Service,
S. S. Superintendent

EXHIBIT 6-D

January 26, 1960

TO ALL TEACHERS AND OFFICERS:

When should a name be removed from the Sunday school roll? This is a question that is frequently asked. Some answers are obvious, such as when a member moves to another city or dies.

In order to standardize and assure a maximum effort to enlist absentees, the teachers and officers agreed at the last meeting to follow this procedure:

1. Ask a class officer or class member to contact the absentee by a visit to try to get interest and attendance.
2. If No. 1 fails to enlist the absentee, then a visit by the class teacher is in order.
3. Should No. 2 fail to get attendance, then the teacher should request the departmental superintendent to visit the absentee.
4. The Sunday school superintendent will visit and lend his assistance if No. 3 does not get results.

In following the above, we assure ourselves and others that a sincere Christian love is shown in wanting all to have an opportunity to study God's word and have fellowship with other Christians.

When this procedure fails, then the superintendent will remove a name from the roll upon request of the teacher.

S. S. Superintendent

EXHIBIT 6-E

January 26, 1960

TO ALL TEACHERS, OFFICERS, and CLASS SECRETARIES:

How should a class record book be marked? When is a student qualified for an attendance award?

At the January planning meeting, the teachers and officers requested that all standardize and use the following symbols and system:

P—use this symbol to indicate presence of a class member
A—use this symbol to indicate absence of a class member
S—use this symbol to indicate sickness as cause of absence
V—use this symbol to indicate vacation or attendance at another church school

The symbols "S" and "V" are intended primarily for use in those classes of children and youth where records are kept for attendance award purposes. In this case it is preferred that you only pencil in "A" lightly until it is known whether a "V" or "S" is the appropriate symbol. A note from a parent or a phone call to a parent, or an attendance card from another church school is needed to change an "A" to another symbol. This should be done within the same month period in which the absence occurs.

To be eligible to receive an attendance award or pin, the Christian Education Board has established a standard which allows four absences per year for vacation or sickness when reported as outlined above.

S. S. Superintendent

EXHIBIT 6-F

SUNDAY SCHOOL

Three-teacher work cycle for two-hour periods in nursery, primary, and kindergarten:

1. Teacher—Name—as example A
2. Teacher—Name—as example B
3. Teacher—Name—as example C

	Teachers for	
	First Hour	Second Hour
September 27	A & B	A & B
October 4	A & B	A & C
October 11	A & B	A & C
October 18	B & C	B & C
October 25	B & C	B & A
November 1	B & C	B & A
November 8	C & A	C & A
November 15	C & A	C & B
November 22	C & A	C & B
November 29	A & B	A & B
December 6	A & B	A & C
December 13	A & B	A & C
December 20	B & C	B & C
December 27	B & C	B & A
1960 January 3	B & C	B & A
January 10	C & A	C & A
January 17	C & A	C & B
January 24	C & A	C & B
January 31	A & B	A & B

EXHIBIT 6-G

1959-1960 CLASSROOMS
STARTING OCTOBER 1, 1959
DOWNSTAIRS

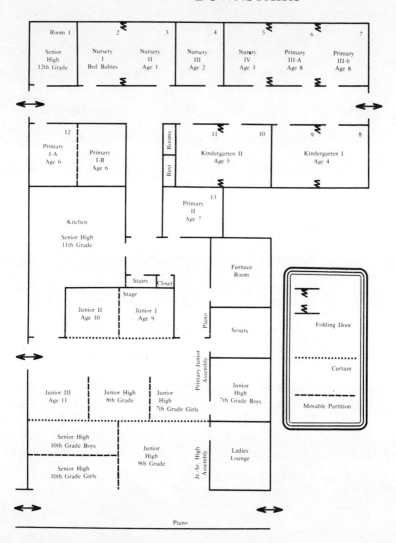

146

EXHIBIT 6-H

NURSERY POLICIES APPROVED

The overall purpose of the Nursery ministry is to meet the needs of each child, especially his spiritual needs. Nursery teachers accept the joint responsibility of home and church, seeking to provide Bible learning experiences that will aid each child in his growth toward a mature Christian personality.

In an effort to improve this ministry, the church in conference approved the nursery policies on July 21, 1968, as recommended by the Nursery Committee. The three main purposes of the policies are

1. to provide a safe, quiet, happy environment for nursery age children on every occasion when they are at the church;
2. to promote understanding between parents and teachers; and
3. to enlist cooperation on the part of the entire church to better meet the needs of nursery children.

The following are a few of the policies most pertinent to our entire church family. (Copies of the entire policies as approved are available in the church office.)

1. In order to provide the safest environment in our departments, children older than nursery age are not permitted in a nursery department.
2. The nursery departments shall be provided for all special churchwide activities. Provision for organizational, divisional, sectional, and departmental activities is without charge.
   a. Individual classes, unions, or circles desiring nursery facilities may reserve the nursery and pay the necessary charges.
   b. Any person or group desiring to use the nursery facilities should notify the children's director three days in advance so that workers can be secured.
3. The nursery shall be open fifteen minutes before each scheduled meeting and shall remain open for fifteen minutes following each meeting.
   a. For evening activities, the nursery shall remain open no later than 10:00 P.M.
   b. In order that the departments be clean and ready for Sunday, provision for nursery children cannot be made on Saturday.

EXHIBIT 6-I

LOCAL CHURCH OPPORTUNITIES
FOR LEADERSHIP EDUCATION

One of the crying needs of the church today is for more and better trained leaders. Whereas it may be difficult to find leaders, there is no reason why any church should neglect the training of either its present or potential leaders.

"The degree to which a leader applies himself to preparation indicates the measure of his consecration." In order that local leadership may be challenged and trained, American Baptists have built a splendid program of leadership education. There are many opportunities for informal training for which the student receives no credit. However, it is hoped that local churches will plan an ongoing program of leadership education built around First and Second Series Leadership Education courses, for which credit is earned. The following types of leadership education opportunities are purely suggestive, but may provide help as you plan your own program:

1. *Week night.* A local church class or school meeting on a week night might be related to the midweek prayer service, or a church night program, or a school of missions. An effective arrangement is one or more classes which meet for a single session each week (five or six weeks for First Series credits,* ten or twelve weeks for Second Series credits**).

2. *Monthly workers' conference.* Of the nine or more monthly workers' conferences held during the year, at least six consecutive sessions of fifty minutes each may be given to the teaching of a course.

3. *Sunday morning class.* A class for prospective teachers and leaders can be organized as a part of the regular Sunday church school. Where a class or classes are held regularly on Sunday morning for at least thirteen weeks, it is possible to provide a definite and continuous program of leadership education. Some youth and adult classes wish to depart from the uniform lessons for a time and devote a series of weeks to elective courses offered for credit.

4. *Sunday afternoon or evening.* Sunday afternoon or evening classes or schools offer opportunities for those unable to attend at other times.

5. *Community schools.* The local church should urge its workers to attend community leadership education schools held in the vicinity. Some churches encourage regular attendance by paying the registration fee or by providing the textbooks for each worker.

6. *Summer conferences.* The summer offers opportunities to young

148

people for leadership education in assemblies and vacation church schools.

7. *Home study.* Here is a plan available to everyone over sixteen years of age having completed the tenth grade. This plan makes it possible for an individual to take a leadership education course through correspondence with the national office.

* First Series requirements: A minimum of five fifty-minute periods in class (six is better) with an equal amount of time in outside study. Approved courses and texts are listed in First Series leaflet.

** Second Series requirements: A minimum of ten fifty-minute class sessions (twelve is better) with an equal number of hours spent in outside work. Approved texts and courses are found in the Second Series leaflet.

EXHIBIT 6-J

MINISTER OF EDUCATION, OR
ASSISTANT PASTOR—EDUCATION, OR
DIRECTOR OF EDUCATION

EDUCATION
QUALIFICATION
Should be a graduate from an accredited college and an ordained graduate in Education of a Baptist seminary or an acceptable equivalent through a combination of education and experience.

AGE
Emphasis will be placed on ability to do the job rather than age, although preference would be shown for the person with most of his career ahead instead of behind.

GENERAL
Either male or female.

JOB
DESCRIPTION
A full-time job of developing the entire education program, except music, of the church and coordinating these activities within the total church program for the spiritual and cultural enrichment of the entire membership through corporate study or individual or group participation.

The following is intended to illustrate the type of activities to be performed but will not be all-inclusive:

1. Serve as a resource and catalyst in developing a fully graded Bible study program in the Sunday school in cooperation with the church school superintendent.
   (a) Coordinate promotion of the Sunday school program through the appropriate organizations of the church.
   (b) Do visitation as needed to assist in enlistment of lay leadership.
   (c) Analyze the need for and assist in developing leadership training programs.
2. Serve in a similar capacity as above in relation to
   (a) The Sunday Evening Training Union program
   (b) The Christian Service Brigade
   (c) The Pioneer Girls
   (d) The Guild Girls
   (e) Any other educational organization that may be initiated other than music.

150

3. Work with appropriate lay leadership in promoting and developing a camping program within Peters Creek Baptist through our American Baptist camps.
4. Serve in capacity similar to no. 3 above, with the elected athletic director of the church in promoting and developing a wholesome recreation and athletic program.
5. Cooperate with the pastor and any other church staff or lay leadership in developing new or improved methods or educational opportunities that will result in greater knowledge of the Bible, spiritual maturity, and service oriented membership.
6. Participate in worship or special services as an individual or through leadership of especially prepared groups.
7. Cooperate with the pastor and any other church staff to assist in the success of the entire church program.

ORGANIZATION RELATIONSHIP The minister of education, like all professional staff, will report and be responsible to the pastor of the church.

EXHIBIT 6-K

MINISTER OF MUSIC

EDUCATION QUALIFICATIONS	Should be a music major from an accredited college and an ordained graduate of a Baptist seminary or an acceptable equivalent through a combination of education and experience.
AGE	Emphasis will be placed on ability to do the job rather than age, although preference would be shown for a person with most of his career ahead instead of behind.
GENERAL	Either male or female.
JOB DESCRIPTION	A full-time job of developing the entire music program of the church and coordinating these activities within the total church program for the spiritual and cultural enrichment of the entire membership through corporate worship or individual participation.

The following is intended to illustrate the type of activities to be performed but will not be all inclusive:

1. Develop a graded choir program that will include all age groups.
   (*a*) Coordinate the promotion of the music program through the appropriate organizations of the church.
   (*b*) Do visitation as needed to promote and enlist membership in the music program.
   (*c*) Enlist the necessary lay leadership to assist in the music program.
   (*d*) Conduct necessary rehearsals.
2. Provide individual or group instruction and training as needed and as time permits to develop individual musical talents of members enlisted in the music program so that soloists or special groups are available to support the total church program, as needed.
3. Participate in worship or special services by providing and leading the appropriate choir, choirs, soloist or special groups, as needed.
4. Cooperate with the pastor and any other church staff to assist the success of the entire church program.
5. Encourage and promote the development of instrumentalists and instrumental groups for service within the church organization.

152

ORGANIZATION RELATIONSHIP The minister of music, like all professional staff, will report and be responsible to the pastor of the church. Any personnel assisting with the music program will be supervised by the minister of music.

EXHIBIT 6-L

SUNDAY SCHOOL
SIX POINT INDIVIDUAL REPORT

Name_____ Sunday_____
If *Visitor* Give
Home Address _____

Class_____ Amount of Offering $_____

Check (√) each point attained and add up total grade.

Attendance 20%	On Time 10%	Bible Brought 10%	Offering 10%	Prepared Lesson 30%	Preaching Attendance 20%	Total Grade
√	√	√	√	√	√	*100*

Visits Made___*8*___ Phone Calls___*6*___ Letters & Cards___—___ Total Contacts___*14*___

Code 4388-02, Form 25, Broadman Supplies, Nashville, Tennessee, Printed in U. S. A.

154

VII

Recreation

A status symbol is an instrument you clash when you want someone to know you are there.

William Sansom

One of the major changes in society in the past several years is the increase in leisure time. This trend will continue. This increase is due to a shorter workweek and also to fewer years because of later entry and earlier exit from the work force. The organized church has generally made an insufficient effort to help its members find useful ways to occupy this free time. Because the church has not acted aggressively in this area, and because increased affluence has made it easier for people to choose from a variety of possibilities, it has become a "double negative" to the church. First, the church has lost a great opportunity to use these interesting and wholesome activities as a means of attracting people to the church. Second, these same activities which are so attractive have been pursued personally, by individuals, and commercially, in a manner that has led people away from the more traditional worship and educational activities of the church, because the mobility takes them away from the church building on weekends.

Some individual churches have done something about it—particularly the large churches. Every church can do something, but the smaller churches may need to join forces to increase their effectiveness. Again, as has been the theme of this book, good planning and professional implementation of the plans is the key to success. Every good plan has a purpose and objective that must be clearly communicated and understood. This principle is illustrated by the following policy statement used by a church that has been successful in the leisure time area as well as its total program.

POLICIES FOR CHURCH RECREATION CENTER

The purpose of the Church Recreation Center of the church is to provide creative and meaningful leisure time activities for its members and guests in a Christian atmosphere and setting. This program is an integral part of the total ministry of the church and seeks to complement, undergird, and strengthen all of our ministries and organizations. Emphasis will be placed upon leading individuals to our Lord and Savior, Jesus Christ, as well as helping Christians grow and mature in their faith.

I. Membership or Eligibility for Participation in the Recreation Program
   A. All members of the church, or any member of its Sunday school, choirs, and other church-sponsored organizations are eligible for participation privileges.
   B. All children and youth, ages four through eighteen years of age, who meet the above membership requirements, are required to complete a PARTICIPATION APPLICATION (signed by parents) and return it to the Office of the Minister of Recreation before they may participate in the programs offered by the Recreation Center.
   C. Each child or young person will be issued an ACTIVITIES CARD which will be kept on file in the Recreation Center. Each time the participant comes to the Center, he will receive his card to use while in the building to check out equipment and games. The card is returned to the receptionist upon leaving the Center.
   D. ACTIVITIES CARDS are not transferable.
II. Guests of Members
   A. Each registered member is entitled to bring two guests with him to the Center without obtaining special permission. A telephone call to the Minister of Recreation is necessary to approve more than two guests.
   B. A sponsoring member is responsible for their guest's conduct at all times while inside the Center.

156

C. Each guest must complete a VISITOR'S CARD before he enters the activity area.

D. The guest may leave without the member; however, if the member leaves, the guest must leave also.

III. Reservations

A. All reservations are to be made through the Office of the Minister of Recreation. (Forms provided.)

B. Only church groups or organizations and other church-related groups may reserve any part of the Recreation Center.

C. All groups requesting reservations must provide adequate adult supervision with children and youth activities.

D. Reservations should be made at least two weeks in advance. The facilities shall be relinquished upon termination of reserved time.

E. Reservations should be promptly cancelled if plans are changed.

F. The use of the Center, facilities, or equipment by nonaffiliated groups is subject to the approval of the Board of Deacons.

IV. General Regulations

A. Smoking will not be allowed in the Center.

B. Pets should not be brought into the Center.

C. Eating or drinking will not be allowed in the gymnasium at any time. The Snack Area is reserved for this purpose.

D. The Center will not be used during regularly scheduled church services, and will be closed fifteen minutes prior to all services.

E. All boys and girls four (4) through eight (8) years of age must be accompanied by an adult at all times while in the Center, unless prior arrangements have been made with the Minister of Recreation.

F. At least one parent must accompany children under eighteen years of age on Family Night (2nd and 4th Friday of each month) during the entire time.

G. The church Recreation Center is a part of the church, and everyone should conduct himself accordingly.

H. The Minister of Recreation will be responsible for the interpretation and enforcement of these rules under the direction of the Recreation Committee and the Board of Deacons.

The importance of this policy statement for your consideration is not whether you agree or disagree with its total contents. Its important points are as follows:

1. It shows that this particular church has *planned* and spent considerable money to provide both facilities and program for leisure time use.
2. The entire family was considered and cared for in the planning.
3. Policies have been established in writing and someone has been made responsible for implementing the policy.
4. Nonmembers can use the program; but to do so, a member must be involved (outreach).
5. And most importantly, it is operated as a part of the church to undergird and strengthen all our ministries and organizations. Emphasis will be placed upon leading individuals to our Lord and Savior, Jesus Christ, as well as helping Christians grow and mature in their faith.

Follow these principles and you will add to the effectiveness of your own church's efforts. Obviously, if you are large enough to own and operate facilities of your own, you are fortunate. Smaller churches with initiative and desire can use a combination of the church building, community playground, and local public school facilities. Leadership, organization, and scheduling make this possible, as has been demonstrated by many churches. Do not try to implement these suggestions on the spur of the moment, because such an effort will only lead to frustration and failure. *Plan.* Create a vision of a desire for what can be done; then do it with vigor and enthusiasm.

Every church situation is not identical; so you must in your planning take into consideration the interests and desires of the people as well as what is possible. Do not try to do so many things that none are done well; but on the other hand, do not dismiss the subject by concluding it is not possible to do anything, because we all can do something. Here are some activities to consider and choose from.

1. *Site of church building*
   (*a*) Inside—In addition to the host of recreational game activities, this category may also include athletic games such as basketball, volleyball, Ping-Pong, and others if you have a gymnasium or have planned well enough to have a combination facility. It also includes organized educational activities

such as Scouting, Pioneer Girls, golden age clubs, and social activities.

(b) Outside—activities in this category tend to be athletic in nature. They include activities such as baseball and softball, picnic facilities, gardening, and the maintenance of church facilities.

2. *Away from site of church building*

(a) Inside—Athletics, recreation, camping, and a variety of educational, inspirational services and pleasurable activities are included.

(b) Outside—Camping, recreation, athletics, Scouting, and a variety of service activities are included.

This list is not intended to be all-inclusive; nor is it intended to suggest that each church organization should attempt to implement each activity. Know your congregation and community needs so well that you can match them through the proper selection of just the right activities. Be prepared to change emphasis from time to time. One example will be used here to illustrate the importance of keeping up with the changing environment and changing these programs accordingly.

Camping is an activity engaged in by a large number of churches and church organizations for many years. Camping probably has been about as universal as any of the activities suggested above. Yet camping as practiced by most church organizations has been on the decline for years and today is in a deplorable state of affairs—not because people no longer are interested in camping, but because church groups have not recognized the need for change or have been too parochial in their views to permit an atmosphere in which change is possible.

Take, for example a church organization in which camping had gotten major emphasis for years. Back when transportation was slow and difficult, camping facilities were created in six different parts of the state involved. Approximately 1,500 acres of land were involved, which have a value today of at least $1,500,000. With an investment for modest but totally inadequate facilities and operating programs, this group had more invested in camping than in any other activity, with the exceptions of "houses of worship" or "foreign mission support." If one had taken a vote of the 100,000 constituents of this group, camping certainly would not have rated a priority commensurate with the investment. This was true for two reasons. First, a survey was made of a large sample of the constituency to find out; and second, attendance was steadily declining for ten years and was down to 1,400 annually. Operating subsidies had reached $75,000 annually. What went wrong? Several things.

1. Society became more affluent.
2. Affluence brought on a greater desire for comfort and convenience.
3. Affluence and an interstate highway system brought mobility of society.
4. Commercial institutions recognized change and acted to meet the desires of society for comfort and convenience with modern, mobile campers and other leisure facilities with higher health and safety standards and programs that were attractive and appealing.
5. Church organizations generally did not upgrade either facilities or program, because they did not recognize change and inadequate financing of proliferated facilities.
5. Since camps tended to be developed historically by local groups for local groups, few have been willing to dispense with "their own" to pool with others to provide what their people would support.

A breakthrough has now been made. As a result of analysis, one group grasped the above points and concluded that pooled resources for a high quality facility and a new program was the only answer—a year-round facility that could involve the interests of all family members with a variety of activities from camping to conferences under a new label: Christian Outdoor Education. Two properties have been sold. A third of the six is for sale. Studies and planning are now underway to determine the precise plan to follow to meet the needs so this activity can again become an effective tool of the church.

Incidentally, if you have a camping problem, or are considering its use in your programs, the following comments of Ernest F. Schmidt, executive director of the American Camping Association, are worth your consideration.

LET'S TAKE A LOOK INTO THE 1970'S

The tasks of any Association Executive are: 1) To protect, guide, supply, represent and inform his people; 2) To administer his association so as to effectively and efficiently accomplish the association's goals; 3) To establish good relationships with organizations and agencies which might affect his association or his people.

These things this Executive Director strives hard to do. But more and more camping people are asking me questions in a very different dimension—the FUTURE! Although we have no crystal ball at ACA Headquarters, we do have something far better—we have *contacts*.

Bradford Woods is *the* focus and clearinghouse for camping information and action for the whole country. So the step from present to future becomes one of analysis and interpretation. Some trends are clearly evident right now; others are nebulous. But let's take a look into the 1970's . . .

There will be fewer camps and they will be larger. This trend began about 10 years ago and seems to be continuing. *There will be more specialized camps*—for high adventure, for special children, handicapped, educational camps. *There will be consolidation in management* with camps using joint bookkeeping services, promotional services, etc. Perhaps there will even be chains of camps across the country.

There will be better leaders, more highly trained. Leaders with open minds, who are flexible and highly skilled.

There will be a greater demand for quality and safety. The ACA accredited camp sign will be harder to get and harder to keep and will attain a much higher degree of recognition by the general public.

There will be less land available for camping and it will have a higher price tag. *There will be joint use of land and longer seasons.* More camps will be spreading their investment from a short 60 days to perhaps 360 days. This trend is particularly important for it will force the winterization of many camping facilities, and renovation and modernization of older camps. Communities giving money for agency camps may demand fuller use of those facilities and perhaps a community share in their use.

There will be far more government involvement in camping on the local, state, and federal levels. Taxes and regulations of all kinds will increase. ACA Section Legislative Committees will attain an importance never realized in the past. *Companies, corporations or agencies will operate more camps; private owners, fewer.* But both the teams and the individuals will be of a far higher quality and calibre than in the past. *And good, topnotch private camps have a bright future.*

There will be more competition for campers, and for camping. Camping people are going to have to vigorously defend and sell camping and its values. Camping is going to have to become more "relevant"—a word I'm not at all sure I like, for it actually is not a concrete term but exists only in the mind of the listener. But the camp which neglects teaching its campers the values and skills of ecology and environmental quality won't be around tomorrow.

Nor will camps which, to quote Howard Gibbs, a former ACA National president, "claim to have 30 years of experience when actually they had only one year repeated 30 times." *Tomorrow's camp director will be intelligent, thoroughly trained, a careful administrator, a fine PR person—and above all, dedicated to children.*

Well, these are a few brief glimpses into what is most surely coming. A terrifying look? Not at all, but rather a tremendous challenge. ACA and its National Board are active in all areas right now. A camp director, alone, can be a pretty lonely guy. With ACA, he's 10 feet tall! Together, we'll be ready!

The goal of Christian outdoor education as stated by the group whose activities were referred to earlier is quoted as follows:

OUR GOAL—CHRISTIAN GROWTH

The objective of Christian Outdoor Education (Camping) includes both evangelism and discipleship. It is to supplement and augment the local church's Christian Education ministry. It is doing that which can best be done in the out-of-doors.

It is life centered in the true sense of the word. Every individual becomes involved as a participant. This involves sharing responsibilities, involved as a participant. This involves sharing responsibilities, expressing love in action, evaluating one's own motives, practicing forgiveness. It is an outdoor workshop of Christian living which helps to bridge the gulf between academically known Christian beliefs and real-life situations.

This ministry provides hope for personal renewal and growth to all ages and groupings. It also becomes an avenue for unique and significant mission opportunities through which the church shares the love of Christ to persons of special need, such as the mentally retarded, the physically handicapped, the inner city disadvantaged, the socially disadvantaged, and others.

If you think this has been a chapter on camping, we have failed you. Camping was used as a specific example to illustrate two points:

1. The need to continually analyze the environment, plan, and implement professionally each activity of your church program.
2. The need to have programs in your church for recreation, athletics, camping, etc, as one means of constructively utilizing leisure time and helping to focus attention on the purposes of the church.

Activities in the leisure area should be a part of the church and aimed at accomplishing the objectives of the church. Viewed and pursued in any other manner, they are in competition with commercial ventures and almost sure to fail.

VIII

Worship—Fellowship—
Prayer—Pastoral Care

*My personal job is to shape my conduct so that it would pro-
mote the well-being of mankind as a whole if everyone followed
my example.*

Robt. A Millikan

Mention the word *church* and the first image flashing into most
people's minds is a building where people go to worship. The second
most likely thought is of that which happens in those buildings
across the country at approximately 11:00 A.M. on Sunday
mornings—listening to a "sermon," a choir, participating in prayer,
singing, communion, offerings, baptism, announcements; or "nap"
time. It is the worship-fellowship-prayer experience, whether
scheduled on Sunday morning, evening, or at various other times
and on special occasions, about which we are thinking here.

Worship

Give unto the Lord the glory due unto his name: bring an
offering, and come before him: worship the Lord in the beauty
of holiness. (1 Chron. 16:29)

Make a joyful noise unto the Lord, all ye lands. Serve the Lord
with gladness: Come before his presence with singing. Know ye
that the Lord he is God: It is he that hath made us, and not we

ourselves; we are his people, and the sheep of his pasture. Enter into his gates with thanksgiving, and into his courts with praise: be thankful unto him, and bless his name. (Ps. 100:1-4)

The Lord is in his holy temple: let all the earth keep silence before him. (Heb. 2:20)

I will therefore that men pray every where, lifting up holy hands, without wrath and doubting. (1 Tim. 2:8)

Thou shalt worship the Lord thy God, and him only shalt thou serve. (Luke 4:8)

Not forsaking the assembling of ourselves together, as the manner of some is; but exhorting one another: and so much the more as you see the day approaching. (Heb. 10:25)

Again I say unto you, that if two of you shall agree on earth as touching anything that they shall ask, it shall be done for them of my Father which is in heaven. For where two or three are gathered together in my name, there am I in the midst of them. (Matt. 18:19-20)

When we think about the meaning of these words and picture the scene in our minds and compare it to what happens in most of our churches, perhaps a little insight can be gained on why attendance continues to slip. The Sunday morning worship is usually the first exposure a newcomer or visitor has to a church. It is, therefore, extremely important that three things happen during this encounter. First, a truly worshipful atmosphere should exist. Second, each activity taking place should be done well. A thoughtful and professionally presented sermon, music—solo or choir—also should indicate ability and preparation. Third, a warm and friendly atmosphere should exist. A friendly greeting on arrival, assistance with coats in winter months, and help in seating preferably near someone who will speak to the visitor at the conclusion.

What kind of schedule or sequence of events should be included in a worship experience? Although there may be a necessity for a basic pattern that will be followed most of the time and that will appeal to a particular congregation, we suggest there be freedom to try variations. In any endeavor of the church, freedom to follow the leading of the Holy Spirit may dictate deviation from the usual pattern on some occasions. The important point is that planning and preparation are essential to doing our best, and nothing less than our best should be thinkable in the Lord's work.

It is easier to illustrate what not to do sometimes than it is to illustrate what to do; so both approaches will be used here.

1. Start at the appointed time. Do not start late.

2. Make the auditorium available for seating at least fifteen minutes prior to starting time. Do not have a flurry of activity going on during this period. This conveys the impression of inadequate prior preparation and prevents the quiet period of meditation needed in preparation for worship.

3. Use the familiar to develop a unity of spirit early in the worship, whether through song, scripture, or prayer. Do not use at this time, for example, a song for congregational singing that may be unfamiliar to many worshipers.

4. Promote, in the form of announcements from the pulpit, only those things of highest priority in the church or community affairs, because these "little" things tend to tell more about your church and you than most realize. Do not try to announce everything going on and do not announce anything that has not been thoughtfully planned in advance. Some pastors who do a beautiful job in delivering a sermon they have worked on and prepared in advance will be totally disorganized and stutter and stammer through an announcement period simply because they are not prepared and are trying to think it out as they go. This can disrupt a worship atmosphere and turn off minds that need the message to follow.

5. Pastors, be prepared so that the sermon comes through as though you believe it important. Most people speak with *conviction* about things they believe in. Do not bring a message "just because it is an "in" thing." The best-known preacher in town will be emphasizing it.

6. Pastors, keep the length of your message within the attention span of your people. TV and other communications experiences have conditioned most to a relatively short span. Do not make a habit of going on longer, but do not hesitate to keep speaking if you feel a strong leading of the Holy Spirit to do so on occasion. If speaking overtime happens frequently, perhaps you should try harder to be led by the Spirit during preparation.

7. Pastors, insist on rehearsing others who participate in leading any portion of worship. Hopefully you will not be asking them to do more than you are doing. Do not think that rehearsal is only for you and the choir.

Communion is one example. An outline in writing should be given each person assisting in this worship ordinance. Then it should be rehearsed. Exhibit 8-A at the end of this chapter is one example of communicating on this subject. Whatever your communion procedure, use this technique so that it will be done in a quiet and worshipful atmosphere. In some larger churches, in particular, it is not unusual to see a deacon lose his correct position and inadvertently create a distraction. In other situations observed, communion has become such a mechanical ritual in the way and speed with which it is served that it ceases to be a worship experience and becomes an interlude of whispering.

Baptism is another ordinance that should be rehearsed with participants. This is especially true where immersion is used. Seeing a pastor trying to immerse a tall or heavy person and having the scene seem a reenactment of a drowning is neither conveying the worshipful message intended nor encouraging others who may be contemplating baptism. Apparently some seminaries do not demonstrate the following technique.

First Sequence

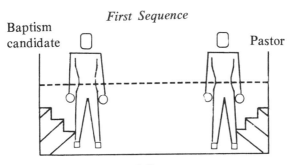

Baptism candidate

Pastor

Second Sequence

Baptism candidate in
squatting position
in water up to neck.
Pastor erect.

Third Sequence

Candidate continues squatting
in water but with pastor
tilting candidate's head backward
to immerse.

Fourth Sequence

Both erect.

8. Pastors, keep the purpose of that which you schedule as worship just that—worship. Do not use these occasions to let your sermon become a response to a debate between you and a parishioner or to "fight back" at those that seem to be against you. On too many occasions, one can predict next Sunday's sermon if there has been a conflict within the fellowship that week. This is not to suggest that the pastor should not have a message or thought concerning conflict, but only that most conflicts can be handled more effectively outside the pulpit and that these conflicts generally are outside the basic purpose of worship.

9. Do provide facilities and attendants to care for nursery children and others too young to meaningfully participate in a worship experience. Do not insist that this group include ages above kindergarten unless you are providing a separate, meaningful worship experience for them. Certainly by the age of attendance in public school, children should be learning the personal discipline and meaning of worship. It is not a bad idea to let them see the example of their parents at worship and for parents to feel a responsibility to help them learn.

10. Provide a sound or closed circuit video system to bring the worship to nursery workers. Provide a rotation system, as described in the chapter on education, so that no worker has to go for extended periods of time without being in the midst of the worship.

11. Ushers play a role far more important than that of just seating people and taking the collection. Lighting, heat, ventilation, and a whole variety of factors that affect the comfort, atmosphere, and

attitude of the assembled worshipers can be controlled or significantly influenced by ushers. Every usher should receive training in the responsibilities of the job and should be expected to perform accordingly. Rather than go into detail here, the reader is referred to *A Guide to Church Ushering* by Homer J. R. Elford, published by Abingdon Press.

Fellowship is a term that is often used in church circles. Most frequently the reference will be to a social affair or an event involving a meal. The definition of fellowship is the condition of being together or of *sharing* similar *interests* or *experiences;* the companionship of individuals in a congenial atmosphere and *on equal terms;* a union of friends or *equals* sharing similar interests. Viewed in this context, virtually every activity within the church, when conducted in a truly Christian manner, qualifies as a fellowship. When divisive or unequal in any manner, the activity ceases to be a fellowship, and also ceases to be the powerful force for growth in Christian maturity and service that it otherwise can be.

In other words, any activity pursued by two or more members of a church in a true fellowship will be helpful and serve as a magnet to attract others.

There is no limit to the activities that can qualify as a useful fellowship, so no attempt will be made here to list them. The important thing to accomplish is an understanding of what it means to have a fellowship. One avenue open to all and most useful to the church is to have the leader's families invite two to six families to their homes to get acquainted under fellowship conditions. This practice has been observed for many years. Invite two families of newcomers and two that have been around for a while. A warm atmosphere of feeling a part or wanting to be a part will develop quickly. This creates involvement, which causes growth and maturity.

Prayer

Every activity must be undergirded by prayer. Prayer, however, should not be permitted to become a crutch. Prayer should help each person to be more sensitive to God's leading, so that our talents will be directed where they should be directed. Also, too often, too many people seem to be going through the motions of praying, asking God's guidance in matters for which God had already given talents and abilities with which to find the answers. This seems to be a misuse of prayer. If you are going to make a mistake in prayer, however, then let it be one of commission rather than omission.

Pastoral Care

One of the major reasons a pastor must learn to enlist and use the talents of lay people in the many activities of the church is to relieve the pastor of doing those things that a lay person can do, so that the pastor will have the time to do those things that he must do. The pastor should be the spiritual leader. In this capacity he is expected to prepare and present most sermons or messages at formal worship and many other functions. In addition, there are certain duties that individual members will accept only from the pastor: performing marriages, conducting funerals, and counseling for a variety of social and spiritual problems within families, from broken marriages to drug abuse; sickness; and tragedy.

While deacons can assist with these duties, the pastor cannot abdicate these responsibilities and remain the leader. Therefore, pastors, sit down and estimate how much of your time will be required to do these things that must be done; then you will be better informed and prepared to plan your own activities—those that you must do, and those that you must do through lay people. The most effective and successful pastors first recognize and then do just this.

EXHIBIT 8-A

COMMUNION SERVICE BY THE DEACONS OF CHURCH

Deacons	Chairman	Pastor	V. Chairman	Deacons
1.				1A.
2.				2A.
3.				3A.
4.				4A.
5.				5A.

THE LORD'S TABLE

2 | 1 | 1A | 2A

AUDITORIUM

4 | 3 | 3A | 4A

1. The chairman and vice chairman will lead the deacons from the vestibule to the seats surrounding the Lord's table *upon a nod from the pastor.*
2. The chairman shall indicate when the deacons are to be seated.
3. Upon a signal or word from the pastor, all will rise to serve the bread.
4. The chairman and pastor will pass the trays to the deacons.
5. After all the trays have been passed out, the pastor will be seated and served first by the chairman; then the congregation will be served as shown above. The deacons at position 5 and 5A will serve the balcony.
6. The chairman will serve the choir and organist and then return the plate to the communion table and be seated.
7. When the deacons have served all the congregation, they will return the plates to the pastor and chairman, to be placed upon the table.
8. After the blessing of the wine, the vice chairman and pastor will hand the trays to the deacons. The deacons will rise upon conclusion of the prayer. After the vice chairman has served the pastor, the deacons will serve the congregation. The vice chairman will serve the choir and organist.
9. After all have been served, the deacons will return as before to the Communion table.
10. After the deacons have sat down, they will be served by the pastor.
11. After singing one verse of the Communion hymn, the pastor will lead the deacons from the platform. The pastor will be by himself; the deacons, in pairs. Deacon 5 and 5A will remain at the front of the sanctuary to greet those who have joined with our congregation and those who are leaving from the front to pick up nursery children.

IX

Promotional Methods

The only thing that can be achieved without effort is failure.
Anonymous

"To raise to a more important rank"; "to contribute to the progress or growth of"; "to urge the adoption of"; "to attempt to sell or popularize by advertising or by securing financial support"—these are definitions of the word *promote* as found in a dictionary. How very appropriate are these thoughts when applied to Christianity and what we the church should be doing about it if we are taking the Bible and the teachings of Jesus seriously.

Communications! Communications of our faith in Jesus Christ and all those activities involved in the church designed to demonstrate our faith and cause our growth as Christians should be urged. We must raise Christianity to a more important rank; we must popularize and urge its adoption by others; we must secure financial support. Methods that will improve communications for these purposes for the church are the subject of this chapter.

To have good communications, it is first necessary to understand the answers to these questions:

1. What message do you want to communicate?
2. With whom do you want to communicate?
3. For what purpose do you want to communicate?
4. When is the best time to communicate?
5. What method should be used to communicate?

6. What is the relative importance of the message in comparison to other messages that may seem to have need of communication at the same time?

The answers to questions 1 and 2 are quite obvious. The answer to the third question is either to keep people informed, or to secure a proposed decision or action. Question 4 involves greater judgment; timing is often critical for success. Communicating for informational purposes may be essential for a time before purpose changes to action, and we often change slowly. There may be a need for face-to-face dialogue between individuals privately to develop leadership, understanding, and support for an idea before expanding to larger groups or the masses. "Shooting from the hip," or springing ideas involving significant change, to a group before they are well thought out can be a sure way to a quick burial of the idea. The more important the communication, the more likely is the need for more than one method, involving both sound and sight—and also to schedule without overlap or conflict with another promotion.

For example, a long-range planning report should be discussed orally in a business meeting after it has been presented in written form to each member of the congregation. Also, a communication of this type should be informational in nature, leading to specific actions that would be pursued at a later date, after understanding had been accomplished (see Exhibit 1-A.)

Another example is in the selection and assignment of workers. The following letter was written to a church school worker after considerable personal discussion about the assignment when securing the worker's agreement to serve. This type of communication is best done privately. Note these points in the letter: importance of the job, leadership opportunity, preceding performance reviewed as a challenge, a few suggestions for continued progress, one specific objective, an offer of continuing help.

Dear Sam,
    May I take this opportunity to again thank you for the willingness to be superintendent of the older adult department in Sunday school. Next to the pastor, it is my belief that this job is the most important in the church, because it gives the opportunity to give positive leadership for good to almost the entire adult membership who make the decisions

that decide whether we go forward or backward.

Much progress has been made in the last four years. We have gone from one department to two and from four classes to ten. We have had outstanding teachers and strong spiritual guidance from the department superintendents. Here are some suggestions:

1. Start opening worship promptly at 9:45 A.M. and stop at 10:00 A.M.
2. Make the opening period one of meaningful worship with devotionals led by members of the different classes.
3. Briefly, but with love and enthusiasm, promote
   (*a*) the entire church program
   (*b*) those points of our record system that result in Christian growth and maturity when done.
4. Encourage through individual contact, monthly workers' conference contacts, and visits by each class to conserve and enlist new members.

In addition to the above, we need desperately to start three new classes. One is about ready to start, and Tom _____ is lined up to teach it. I will be glad to work with you on the other two and in any other way possible to further the Lord's work. Both my prayers and energy are available to you. Thanks again for your help and co-operation.

Yours in His service,

The following two reports were given orally as well as in writing to the whole congregation:

SUNDAY SCHOOL REPORT FOR 1959

The church school continued to grow throughout 1959 and had an average attendance of 322 per Sunday. This is 51 per Sunday more than during the previous year 1958. The rate of growth is emphasized by the fourth quarter attendance, which averaged 363 per Sunday or 75 more than in the same period of 1958. Highest attendance any Sunday was 390. Enrollment has reached 550.

During the year, three departments and six additional classes were started. There are now sixty-five teachers and officers working in the school. Teacher-officer meetings are held each month for planning and training purposes, with a high percentage of enthusiastic participation. More than thirty teachers and officers attended a three-night training school conducted by our own Pittsburgh Baptist Association, and ten received educational credit for the course. Two attended the Bucknell lab school.

A very successful vacation Bible school was held under the direction of Mrs._____. The school cooperated with the training union in holding a school of missions.

Because of the excellent cooperation of all teachers, officers, the various church boards, and church staff, the school operated in such a manner that it was possible to make application for an American Baptist Convention Standard of Achievement Award. This application has been approved by the Pittsburgh Baptist Association and is now in ABC headquarters for decision.

Your superintendent wishes to thank all for the wonderful spirit of cooperation received. Special thanks are offered to the adult church membership for the sharply increased attendance in the adult department and the wonderful example it sets for the youth and children of our church and community.

It is my prayer that the Lord may continue to lead us to do an even better job in this important area of Christian education.

Yours in His Service,
Superintendent

SUNDAY SCHOOL REPORT FOR 1960

The church school continued to grow throughout 1960 and had an average attendance of 350 for 51 Sundays. One Sunday in February was snowed out. This compares with an average attendance of 322 in 1959. The rate of growth in 1960 did not keep pace with the high rates set in 1959 or 1958. Enrollment only increased from 550 to 557.

During the year, a new department was formed. This was a middler department for eight- and nine-year-old students. One new adult department class for men was started. This is the King's Men's class which is a counterpart to the long established King's Daughters' ladies' class.

Teacher-officer meetings continue to be held on a monthly basis. This group continues to study to become better servants of our Lord. Two again attended the Bucknell lab school for a week and twenty others earned American Baptist leadership education credits for other study.

Another successful vacation Bible school, and our largest, was held under the joint direction of Mrs. _____ and John _____. The school again cooperated with training union in a school of missions.

Your church school has again been recognized and commended by the American Baptist Convention. A Standard of Achievement Award has been received for the year ending August 31, 1960. This is the second consecutive year to receive this award. Our dedicated teaching staff is to be particularly commended for making the quality of our school such that our school qualified for this award.

Again your superintendent wants to thank our pastor, the various boards, and all others who contributed to the success of the school year. As our community grows, our Christian education responsibility grows. If each of us accept this challenge and go about our task prayerfully, then I am sure the Lord will continue to lead us to greater heights, that through the teaching of the Word, many others may come to know him as Lord and Savior.

Yours in His Service,
Superintendent

Note the positive approach and public commendation and how the second ties in and builds on the first. No, everything was not always good; but constructive suggestions for correcting weaknesses are usually best handled privately.

You will recall the discussion in chapter six of the monthly workers' conference. This is an excellent example of both visual and oral communication in a functional area where the monthly continuity from year to year emphasizes another feature of a good promotional program—repetition. One should continually build on what has happened before. Both memory and anticipation become allies when this is done well. Between such meetings, place in the hands of each worker some written communication to promote private thought. Examples of these follow.

CHECK LIST FOR SELF-EVALUATION OF
TEACHING EFFECTIVENESS

1. The teacher's attitude and understanding of persons in the class.
2. The teacher's preparedness.
3. The teacher's attendance and punctuality.
4. The aim or purpose of the class session.
5. The variety of teaching methods used.
6. The resource background of the teacher.
7. The teacher's response to pupils.
8. The response of the pupils.
9. The discipline of members of the class.
10. Use of the room and equipment in meeting the needs of the pupil and the teacher.
11. Visitation in the home of the pupil once per year.

FORMS TO BE USED IN SELF-EVALUATION

My Growth with Relation to Children

1. Do I make provision for individual differences?
2. Do I make responses to the children at their own level of understanding?
3. Does my relationship to them show that I dominate, mother, or respect them?
4. Is there pupil participation in planning, activities, or evaluation?
5. Are there more children learning to take part?
6. Am I encouraging pupils to think and solve their own problems?
7. Do I record evidences of new pupil growth and make recommendation for further procedure with individuals? With the group?
8. Do the pupils show signs of interest and enthusiasm?

My Growth with Relation to the Teaching Environment

1. Did I do something to make my teaching quarters interesting to the children?
2. Did I use a variety of materials?
3. Did I check to see that materials were available to all?
4. Was the equipment adequate for my plans?
5. Am I creative in making use of all the resources in the teaching setting?
6. Did I anticipate and provide for emergencies?
7. Is the teaching setting organized to take care of early comers, late-comers, administrative interruptions?

My Growth with Relation to the Teaching Process

1. Did the pupils help me to plan their activities for now or later?
2. Did I allow for skills to be developed in areas where they are necessary?
3. Did I at any time interpret what was happening and relate it to everyday life?
4. Did we draw any generalizations which might affect our living together?
5. Was my timing helpful?
6. Did the scheduling contribute to the outcome of the session?
7. Was there a measure of success felt by the teacher? By the pupils?
8. Can I articulate the problems arising from this session?

BEATITUDES FOR TEACHERS

Written by Dr. Paul Warren

Blessed is the teacher who is punctual even at the cost of his Sunday morning sleep, for he says in tones louder than words that Sunday school is important.

Blessed is the teacher who is present regularly, who does not put his own pleasures above the needs of his group, for he is bound to see rich results from his fidelity to his task.

Blessed is the teacher who prepares his lesson early in the week, for he can enjoy his Saturday night and still enjoy his class Sunday morning.

Blessed is the teacher who participates wholeheartedly in the service of worship, for, verily, it will begin to mean something, not only to him, but to his pupils as well.

Blessed is the teacher who secures a substitute when he is forced to be absent and who notifies his superintendent, for such consideration will command the pupils' respect.

Blessed is the teacher who gives his pupils opportunity to take part in the class, for though they may listen politely while he does all the talking, they learn best when they participate.

Blessed is the teacher who uses his imagination in his lesson planning, for he will have a varied program and his pupils will not be bored beyond endurance.

Blessed is the teacher who calls on his pupils, who never wearies in his efforts to win them to their best, for thus he will prove his love for them and make them his friends.

Blessed is the teacher who has a personal knowledge and experience of God, for his Christ-like purity and beauty of character will he best be able to bring others into the Kingdom.

HOW IS YOUR FAMILY GROWING RELIGIOUSLY?

	Poor	Average	Good
1. Grace at meals			
2. Bible reading and prayer together			
3. Devotional booklet made			
4. Erection of "quiet corner" or family altar			
5. Regular purchase of good books of religious or indirectly religious value			
6. Religious pictures in the home			
7. Reading of church paper to keep in touch with the larger affairs of the church and world			
8. Attention to the bulletin of your local church so that the activities of the church are a part of the family planning			
9. Attendance at Bible school and church			
10. Conscious effort in the family fellowship and conversation to bring religious principles to bear upon the concerns of life in home, school, work, and play			

SUGGESTIONS FOR FAMILIES AT WORSHIP

1. *Family Worship*
   Remember God together; thank Him and ask Him for His help and forgiveness. Experiment till you find the best time and way for your family to do this.

2. *Learning to Listen*

   Learn to listen to God when you pray, not just to talk to Him. Does God always have something to say to you? What comes to you from Him when you pray? Cultivate the power of silent, listening prayer.

3. *Let Music Help*

   Can your family use religious music more? Try group singing or a family orchestra or listen together to radio music or phonograph records which help people to worship.

4. *Psalms We Like*

   A family committee might choose some Psalms or parts of Psalms to use together as prayers (Psalms of praise and thanks, Psalms of trust and quiet thought about God, Psalms which ask for help and forgiveness). You might use one Psalm until you all know and love it and then choose another.

Of course, in all these areas of communications, flipcharts, mobiles, dramatic presentations, humorous skits, photographs, and other visual means can be used for variety and emphasis. Special occasions, such as centennials, vacation Bible school, every member canvas or pledge day, preaching missions, and other types of service projects make excellent occasions for effective promotion of God's work both within the church and outside in the community. (See exhibits 9-A, 9-B, and 9-C.)

These special events and church awards also make good opportunities for the use of TV, radio, and newspapers. Many churches broadcast the worship service. These media can be most effective when thoughtfully planned and implemented. When used in any way less than a first quality professional way, a negative result may be obtained. As mentioned elsewhere, Oral Roberts' TV specials set an excellent standard and guideline for anyone planning to use this method. The following is one sample of a news release for a paper.

Leaders of the Peters Creek Baptist Church at Library have been notified that the church has been honored by its denomination. The Board of Education and Publication of the American Baptist Convention has given to this church the 1959 Standard of Achievement Recognition. A bronze plaque and Statement of Recognition has been received from the Baptist Convention by Mr._____, super-

182

intendent of the Peters Creek Church School, who is shown in the photograph presenting it to the Reverend _____, pastor of the church.

This recognition comes to the church because it has attained eleven goals of the Standard of Achievement for American Baptist Sunday Church Schools. The Standard of Achievement consists of twelve goals for the Christian education program; and only those schools which achieve ten, eleven, or twelve goals are eligible to receive this special commendation. It should be noted that only a limited number among the thousands of Sunday church schools in the American Baptist Convention are receiving the coveted recognition.

In speaking of this recognition, the Reverend Mr. _____, pastor of the church, said, "Our superintendent and our teachers and officers, as well as members of our Sunday church school, are to be congratulated on this achievement. They are to be especially commended for their work and devotion. Our church is very grateful to those who have served so faithfully and for the high honor which comes from our denomination."

Keep these brief; if you do, they may be published as you write them. Send in two or three pages, and it will likely be condensed by the editor, who knows little about what you want understood, and it may become a hodgepodge.

While many letters are being used in this chapter for illustration, the thought process contained in them is being emphasized rather than the form. The following examples in the area of finances may be helpful.

"PRAISE GOD FROM WHOM ALL BLESSINGS FLOW"

Truly we should be ever thankful that the Lord is so richly blessing us as a church in these days. Cooperative, consecrated people—new families joining with us—a new parsonage, and brick and wood rapidly going into place in the Sunday school addition.

These outward signs of progress did not "just happen." They are the result of many dedicated people taking a part to make Peters Creek Baptist Church a greater Christian witness for Jesus Christ.

We want this spirit of cooperation to continue as the Lord leads so that every man, woman and child can say, "I have a part in this great program for Christ." It is for this reason that building fund banks have been made available to all children and Sunday, October 18th, designated as Building Fund Day.

Encourage your children to save sacrificially and fill their banks with dimes, quarters, and dollars and be present October 18th to drop their filled banks in the building fund with all the others. This day is for Mother and Dad, too. Let's all pray about this program and then give as the Lord leads. Remember that it is not the few large gifts that mean success, but the many of us giving tithes and sacrificial gifts that will be blessed.

Jesus says in Mark 12:43-44, concerning the two mites (a farthing) cast in by the widow—"Verily I say unto you, that this poor widow hath cast more in than all they which have cast into the treasury: For all they did cast in of their abundance, but she of her want did cast in all that she had, even all her living." Yes, each man, woman, and child can and should have a part in this the Lord's work.

What can we expect of this cooperative effort? Malachi 3:10 tells us, "Bring ye all the tithes into the storehouse, that there may be meat in mine house, and prove me now here with, saith the Lord of hosts, if I will not open you the windows of heaven, and pour you out a blessing, that there shall not be room enough to receive it."

Have a part now by giving regularly each Sunday. Give extra October 18th and make Building Fund Day a great success for His glory. See you in church and about *His* work.

Your Finance Committee

TO ALL MEMBERS:

Subject—Proposed 1960 Budget

Attached hereto your trustee board submits for your consideration a proposed budget for the year 1960. Your attendance at the annual meeting in January is requested to discuss and approve a budget so that the work of the church may be more effectively planned and carried out.

The proposed budget is the result of many hours of study of the needs of the church, related to anticipated income, by the finance committee and your trustee board. Both unanimously recommend this budget to you as meeting all our immediate needs and as being within our financial ability to meet, as demonstrated by expected total 1959

184

income of approximately $40,000.00.

The finance committee was composed of the following:

> Board of Trustees—3 members
> Board of Deacons—1 member
> Board of Deaconesses—1 member
> Board of Christian Education—1 member
> Woman's Mission Society—1 member
> Young People—1 member

This group studied the needs of the various groups and presented recommendations to the Trustee Board, who then finalized the attached proposal.

A bookkeeping system will be set up in accordance with the eleven major headings making up the budget. All expenditures then will be charged and recorded against one of these headings and the appropriate subheading. For example, any expenses connected with vacation Bible school would be against budget item B-4. This will permit a quarterly report to be made to the trustees and congregation of expenditures by accounts compared to the budget.

When approved, many items in the budget, such as salaries, mission gifts and building fund mortgage payments will become known obligations and will be paid automatically each month by the church treasurer. All other items, such as operating expenses, Sunday school literature, etc., are estimated as close as possible to what experience indicates they should be. It will be the responsibility of those currently responsible for expenses in these areas to spend less than the budget calls for, if possible. Responsibility for expenses against the budget and approval of invoices for payment is as follows:

Group A—Salaries—Board of Trustees

Group B—Sunday School—Board of Education approves budget items. Chairman of board or Sunday school superintendent approves invoices.

Group C—Training Union—Same as B except training union director instead of Sunday school superintendent.

Group D—Missionary Society—President mission society approves all invoices.

Group E—Mission Gifts—Items 1, 3, 4, 6, 8 paid by treasurer as invoices received or monthly as indicated. Item 2 paid monthly as received and as designated by giver. Item 5 invoices approved by chairman of deacon board. Items 9 through 15 invoices approved by President of mission society.

Group F—Youth Activity—Invoices approved by board of trustees.

Group G—Music Department—Invoices approved by chairman of music committee.

Group H—Operating Expenses—All invoices except against Item H-6 approved by board of trustees. Item H-6 invoices approved by chairman of deacons or chairman of deaconesses or chairman of the flower committee.

Group J—Building—Approved by building fund treasurer on building contracts—board of trustees on mortgage payments.

Group K—Furniture and Fixtures—Approved by board of trustees.

Group L—Contingent Fund—Approved by board of trustees.

No budget item may be exceeded or items added without prior approval by the board of trustees or the congregation. As provided in the constitution, items under $1,000.00 require only trustee board approval. Nonbudget items larger than this require congregational approval.

As our Christian witness grows, our needs grow; but our membership and income also grow. Total income has been approximately as follows:

Resident Members		$/Member/yr.
339	1957 - $31,000.00	$91.5
384	1958 - $36,000.00	93.8
416	1959 - $40,000.00	96.2
	(based on year to date)	

We will undoubtedly continue to make progress and grow as long as we permit the Lord to use us in His will here in this community. Let us all be in prayer that this will be true so that many more lives may be enriched through the teaching, preaching, training, and mission ministry of this church.

Your Trustee Board and Finance Committee

CAN IT HAPPEN AGAIN?

YES! Because it always happens when a cooperative, thankful people join together in service to the Lord. We, of course, are referring to the very successful Building Fund Day of last year and the Budget and Building Fund Day scheduled for September 18th.

186

Does it need to happen again? Again the answer is *YES!* The total mortgage on the parsonage and educational addition is now $61,700.00. This costs the church $270.00 per month interest. Total monthly expense is $3,200.00 average. All of this is money that has been well spent to further the cause of Christ through our church here in our community and on the mission fields around the world.

Your tithes and offerings each week have been equal to our total expenses, so the Lord has led to meet our needs and we should be thankful. By cooperation and sacrificial giving over and above our weekly effort, however, we can on September 18th bring in a sum which will permit a substantial reduction in the mortgage (and interest savings) while continuing to meet all needs of the church program.

It is for this reason that banks have been made available to all children and Sunday, September 18th, designated as Budget and Building Fund Day. Encourage your children to save sacrificially and fill their banks with dimes, quarters, and dollars, and be present September 18th to drop their filled banks into the miniature church with all the others.

All of you will remember the thrilling experience of children and mothers and dads taking part in this program last year and the "tub of money" ($6,200.00) that was contributed. It is our prayer that this spirit of cooperation continues as the Lord leads so that every man, woman and child can say, "I have a part in this great program for Christ at Peters Creek."

Let's all pray about this program and then give as the Lord leads. Remember that it is not the few large gifts that mean success but the many of us giving tithes and sacrificial gifts that will be blessed.

Will we be blessed? Read Malachi 3:10 and Jesus' words in Mark 12:43-44 and we find that answer is *YES.* Have a part now by giving regularly each Sunday. Give extra September 18th and make this Budget and Building Fund Day a great success for *His* glory.

Your Finance Committee

Displays of books from the church library in a heavy traffic area of the church with an attendant to answer questions can be an effective way to promote the use of the library. If you want teachers to use the reference books as well as films or filmstrips, then make an inventory list and place it in each worker's hands.

CHURCH LIBRARY

35mm Film Strips Available in Library

General
    What Baptists Believe About Baptism   R S
    Ministry of the Deacon S
    Person-to-Person Evangelism R
    What Baptists Feel about Salvation R
    American Baptist Convention (Slides) Detroit
    Walk a New Road S
    Let's Face It S
    Making and Keeping New Friends S
    Learning to Forgive R S
    Christian and His Life Work R S
    Goals for the Church for Children R S For each department
      Plans for Children (Church)
      Nursery Child and the Church
      Kindergarten and the Church
      Primary Children and the Church
      Junior Children and the Church
    Building a Better Sunday School R S Moody Bible Institute
Teaching
    Church Manners R S

Biblical
    Good Tidings to all People R S
    A Cry for Repentance—Jeremiah S
    Escape to Egypt R S
    Resurrection R S
    Babu and the Easter Fair S
    2000 Years Ago S (Series of 6 filmstrips including home—
      traveling—school—work)
    23rd Psalm (Slides taken in Palestine)
    John the Baptist S
    Moody Bible Series of four filmstrips R S Samuel—
      Ahab—Solomon
    How the Bible Came to Us R S 4 parts
    Go Tell the Good News R S Christmas

* S—Script
  R—Recording

At School at Capernaum S (Jesus)
A Trip from Nazareth to Jerusalem S
The Baby King S
Timothy, a Boy from Lyria S

Children's Films
Growing in God's World (Mike Grows) S
A Farmer and His Field S
Tumba of Africa S Teacher's Guide
Leo of Alaska S Teacher's Guide
Mateo of Mexico S Teacher's Guide
The World of Happy Differences S
Sunday Around the World S
So the Kingdom Grows S
Christmas Around the World S R

Missionary Films
One Girl's Story R S
Beyond City Limits R S
With Our Hands R S
Alaska Panorama R S
Latin American Highlights S
The Bible and Diego Thompson S
Pedro and Juanita S
Frank Laubach and Adoniram Judson R S
Adventure in Hong Kong S
Burma Playmates S
One-way Street S
The Hook S
Crossroads at Cedermont S
Philippine Frontiers S
A Day in Nepal S
No Longer a Stranger S
Amerigos Latinos S

Additional Films
The First Americans S
The Users R S Family Management
The Spenders R S Family Management

Biblical
The Prodigal Son S

189

Equipment
    2 small 35mm projectors
    large 35mm projector
    1 small screen
    large screen
    sound projector

All visual aids are a part of the church library and should be checked out, by using the request book on the desk. In this way each one will be able to use films and materials as he needs them.

The well being of the whole should be uppermost in the mind of anyone undertaking any promotional effort in behalf of any part of the church program, and it should be kept centered on the spiritual, as the illustrations used indicate can be done regardless of the functional area involved.

In most churches in the United States today, there is likely to be someone with training in some area of communication who can be enlisted to help the pastor and organizations plan and implement a promotional program. Marketing, advertising, sales, and education are just some of the background areas to look for when seeking help. This background, of course, does not guarantee that a professional job will be done; but the odds certainly should be more in your favor. This person should be a resource to assist in developing the plan of promotion and in producing copy to be used. But this person should not be expected to initiate all individual communication efforts.

Do not let the church bulletin and an occasional newsletter be your primary communications effort. Use them, yes, but not to the exclusion of other methods.

EXHIBIT 9-A

bible time!

lookin' fer ya'

AUGUST 9-13 ✱ AGES 3-15 ✱ 9-11:30 A.M.

All Kids....

YOU ARE WELCOME — CATHOLIC, PROTESTANT, AND JEWISH! BRING ALL THE KIDS IN YOUR NEIGHBORHOOD TO BIBLE TIME!

FIVE FREE GIFTS FIRST DAY AWARDS AND SOUVENIRS

BIBLE TIME USES THE SPIRIT OF COMPETITION AS AN AID TO LEARNING AND OFFERS BEAUTIFUL, LIFETIME ACHIEVEMENT AWARDS AND SOUVENIRS: BALLOONS IN FIVE COLORS, BIBLE TIME BUTTONS, PENS, PENCILS, NEW TESTAMENTS, LOVELY BIBLES, ETC. ALL BOOSTERS WILL EARN AND RECEIVE THESE GIFTS.

SPECIAL TEEN CLASS
(AGES 12-15)

THIS CLASS PLANNED AS TOPS FOR TEENS. THE TEEN LEADER GUARANTEES A TERRIFIC TIME.

FIVE GREAT DAYS!!!
SUMMER FUN
AT ITS BEST

BIBLE TIME IS A PROGRAM THAT IS REALLY DIFFERENT: EMPHASIZING PATRIOTISM, CHARACTER BUILDING, AND BIBLE TEACHING --- WITH PLENTY OF ACTION USING THE MOST MODERN METHODS.

EXCITING

MAGIC - PUPPETS
VISUAL AIDS
COMPETITION

FREE TRANSPORTATION
RIDE A BIBLE TIME BUS OR CAR

IF THIS BROCHURE WAS PRESENTED AT YOUR HOME YOUR AREA IS DESIGNATED FOR FREE TRANSPORTATION. A BIBLE TIME BUS OR CAR WILL PICK YOU UP AT THE CORNER NEAREST YOUR HOME AT 8:30 A.M. AND WILL RETURN YOU HOME AFTER THE RALLY.

BIBLE TIME IS SPONSORED BY THE HIGHLAWN BAPTIST CHURCH, 28TH ST. AND COLLIS AVE., HUNTINGTON, WEST VIRGINIA. REV. FRED V. BREWER, PASTOR. TELEPHONE 522-1282.

GRADUATION NIGHT
SUNDAY - AUG. 15 - 7:00 P.M.

EXHIBIT 9-B

SPECIAL AWARD

MEMORY BOOSTER

bible time '71

HIGHLAWN BAPTIST CHURCH - - Huntington, West Virginia

Enrolled 756   High Day 653   Saved 132

192

EXHIBIT 9-C

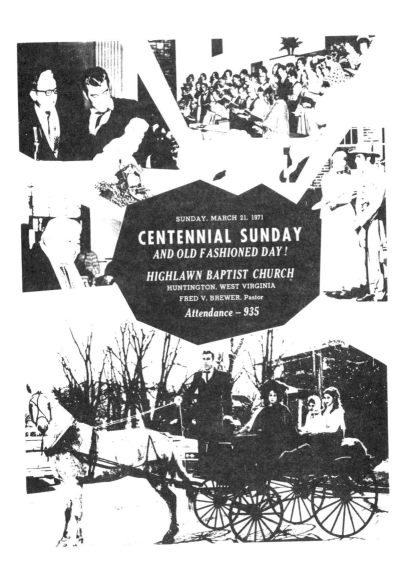

SUNDAY, MARCH 21, 1971

CENTENNIAL SUNDAY
AND OLD FASHIONED DAY!

HIGHLAWN BAPTIST CHURCH
HUNTINGTON, WEST VIRGINIA
FRED V. BREWER, Pastor

Attendance — 935

X

Cooperative Efforts

You may be deceived if you trust too much, but you will live in torment if you do not trust enough.

Frank Crane

Many church groups needlessly restrict the effectiveness of their total programs by not joining forces with other church groups with similar needs when the scope is beyond one group's ability to finance or when it would simply be better stewardship to combine, even if one could handle it. After all, we do say it's God's money, don't we?

Many reasons could be cited for too little cooperative planning and use of facilities, but the two most evident are these:

1. Church people just do not often include this approach as a possible solution when looking at a problem or opportunity.
2. Too often the thinking is that joining forces with another denomination group will result in some kind of contamination of "our" group.

There are enough examples now throughout the country to show that the first should no longer be a reason. Some of these examples will be briefly mentioned later. To those with the second reason— and they often exist within the same denomination—should you not view the situation as an opportunity to bring the "others" up to your own level of spiritual maturity and understanding? Remember

194

Jesus' own example of sitting down with sinners and publicans, for which He was criticized.

He who overcomes others is strong; but he who overcomes himself is mightier.

John H. Patterson

Basic considerations for cooperation should include capital cost, administrative cost, minimum size to be viable as an activity, and the possibility of confusion if pursued individually in an overlapping manner. The most familiar examples of cooperation are as follows:

Missions—This was perhaps the earliest cooperative effort of churches within a given denomination but has made little progress between denominations. It has been most prominent in overseas lands. It is also a domestic effort to help special groups like migrant workers. Christian centers and neighborhood houses used in inner-city ministry are also part of the missions effort.

Housing—Focusing on low-income and senior citizen groups financed under federal government funding.

Hospitals—Health care for the needy and community as a whole.

Camping—Discussed under leisure activities in chapter eight.

Colleges—An early stronghold of the church, more recently abandoned except for the seminary.

Literature—Development of curricular materials and printing.

Staff and Administrative Services—Under this category falls a whole host of services from collecting and remitting funds for mission support to supplying to individual churches, who otherwise could not afford it, professional support in education, administration, personnel selection, and others. These often are performed by the local association or city society.

While many other specific activities could be listed and discussed here, it is not our purpose to write a documentary on cooperation. The purpose is twofold.

First, it is our purpose to call to the attention of any readers who may be lay people that cooperation is an area to be understood and pursued in many areas. Surveys of lay people in many parts of the country show that less than 20 percent of the membership of the local church has any real knowledge or understanding of what the staff of a local association really does or what is the purpose of the association's existence. Lack of understanding leads to divisions and ineffectiveness.

Second, the purpose, objectives, and activities of association staff seldom change over a long period of years, even though the world around may be rapidly changing. Staff of associations rarely initiate change so lay people should be sensitive to the need, and initiate studies from time to time, designed to determine what should be the cooperative objectives of the association.

An effective approach is to form a small committee of lay people and pastors from a representative group of churches, to generally supervise a study designed to determine purposes and objectives that are responsive to the constituents. The procedure followed by the American Baptist Home Mission Societies staff is outlined here.

THE STUDY PHILOSOPHY

The America Baptist Home Mission Societies staff engaged in church and community studies and regional evaluations has in recent years adhered to a philosophy, or a set of principles. Each step is dependent upon the preceding steps.

    a. Mission: Mission is the work of God in reconciliation through Jesus Christ in historic and contemporary life. It is the theological perspective involved in delineating value assumptions on which the life and ministry of the convention is based.

    b. Need: Need is the imperative to Mission and is the description of the sociological or environmental context in which that Mission is to be performed. It is the environmental perspective for assumptions. It needs as objective an analysis as can be achieved. It will be on a selective basis according to the values held in the understanding of Mission.

    c. Purpose: Purpose is the way by which the convention phrases and rephrases its understanding of Mission in light of human need. It must be placed in a context of broad and specific objectives that are measurable.

    d. Resources: Resources limit the selection of purpose and objectives. Resources involve availability of personnel and finances as well as the attitudinal factors of vision, courage and prejudice.

    e. Program: Program is the resultant performance by which purpose is fulfilled and objectives are achieved in light of resources. It is the doing of the Gospel.

    f. Structure: Structure is the form used to fulfill function. It is necessarily a tool designed to change as program changes and as objectives shift in light of changing needs or understanding of Missions.

    g. Personnel: Personnel, employed or volunteer, staff the organization. Personnel are necessarily chosen to bring the requisite skills to the organization in order to carry out the tasks chosen to accomplish the purpose and objectives.

The Strategy Study is designed to help a convention to focus on its specific concerns and also to see those concerns in the perspective of the foregoing philosophy.

Carrying out this philosophy involves in depth research—research in the nature of changes in the community and research in the understanding and desires of the constituents. This is done through personal interviews and written questionnaires. Exhibits 10-A and 10-B show sources of information to be used by the committee to arrive at conclusions and possible new directions for the cooperative efforts to undertake.

No attempt will be made here to show results of a study, only the need and the procedure—a procedure that again emphasizes determining facts, analysis, planning, objectives, and implementation by staff.

Cooperation is desirable, but review from time to time to make sure you are cooperating to accomplish the right things in the best way.

EXHIBIT 10-A

STUDY QUESTIONNAIRE

1973

DEAR ASSOCIATION LEADER:

This form is an important step in the study of program and administration intended to discover ways the Pittsburgh Baptist Association can be even more effective in God's reconciling ministry.

Please complete this form without discussing it with others or referring to any resources. It is your opinion that counts. DO NOT SIGN YOUR NAME. Please answer every question. The information you give is used for statistical purposes only, so your replies will be kept anonymous. Thank you for helping in this way.

1. *Your age* (Please check one.)

   a.——Under 18   c.——25 to 39   e.——50 to 64
   b.——18 to 24   d.——40 to 49   f.——65 or over

2. *Your sex* (Please check one.)

   a.——Male   b.——Female

3. *With whom do you live?* (Check only one.)

   a.——Alone   c.——With spouse and children   e.——Other
   b.——With spouse only   d.——As child with parents

4. *Education* (Check your highest attainment.)

   a.——I am still in school   f.——Completed trade or skill course
   b.——Less than 5 years   g.——Some college
   c.——5 to 8 years   h.——Completed college
   d.——9 to 12   i.——Postgraduate education
   e.——Completed high school   (Degree _____)

5. *In what denomination were you reared as a child?* (Check *only* one.)

   a.——American Baptist   f.——Methodist
   b.——Southern Baptist   g.——Presbyterian
   c.——Disciples of Christ   h.——Roman Catholic
   d.——United Church of Christ   i.——Other (name _____)
   e.—— Lutheran   j.——None

6. *In what type of community did you grow up?* (Check that in which you spent most of your childhood.)

a.——On a farm   d.——City of 10,000 to 49,999
b.——Place of less than 2,500   e.——City of 50,000 or more
c.——Town of 2,500 to 9,999   f.——Suburb of a city of 50,000 or
                                      more

7. *In what type of community do you live now?*

a.——On a farm   d.——City of 10,000 to 49,999
b.——Place of less than 2,500   e.——City of 50,000 or more
c.——Town of 2,500 to 9,999   f.——Suburb of a city of 50,000 or
                                      more

8. *Present status* (Check only one.)

a.——Homemaker   c.——Employed   e.——Unemployed
b.——Student   d.——Retired

9. *If now employed, what is your type of work?*

a.——Professional
b.——Technical
c.——Manager or administrator
d.——Owner or proprietor
e.——Clerical
f.——Machine operator
g.——Other (specify) _____

10. *If now employed, what is your place of work?*

a.——Government
b.——Education
c.——Retail/wholesale trade
d.——Service
e.——Industry
f.——Farming
g.——Other (specify) _____

11. *What was your total family income last year?*

a.——Under $3,000   d.——$10,000 to $14,999
b.——$3,000 to $4,999   e.——$15,000 to $19,999
c.——$5,000 to $9,999   f.——$20,000 to $29,999
                           g.——$30,000 or more

12. *How many contribute to the total income reported above?*

    a.——One   b.——Two   c.——Three or more

13. *Housing you live in* (Check only one.)

    a.——Single family dwelling   d.——Nursing or retirement home
    b.——Apartment   e.——Dormitory
    c.——Mobile home   f.——Other (Specify ———————)

14. *Do you rent or own your home?*

    a.——Rent   b.——Own   c.——Other ———————————

15. *About what age were you when you first joined a church?*

    a.——11 or under   c.——Older than 15, but under 21
    b.——12 through 15   d.——21 or over

16. *How long have you been a member of this church?*

    a.——Less than 1 year   d.——5 to 10 years
    b.——1 to 3 years   e.——10 to 20 years
    c.——3 to 5 years   f.——Over 20 years

17. *Generally speaking, how often do you attend the following in your church?* (Check *after each type* of activity.)

NOTE: Cross out the meetings your church does not have:

	3 or more per month	Twice monthly	Once monthly	Less often	Never
a. Major worship	——	——	——	——	——
b. Other worship	——	——	——	——	——
c. Mid-week service	——	——	——	——	——
d. Church school	——	——	——	——	——
e. Men-women-youth or mixed group meeting	——	——	——	——	——
f. Board of committee	——	——	——	——	——

18. *In which of the following other activities of YOUR church do you participate regularly?* (Check as many as apply.)

NOTE: Cross out the meetings your church does not have:

    a.——Special study groups—not the church school
    b.——Special prayer groups—not the mid-week service

c.——Family nights
d.——Social action group
e.——Retreats for church leaders
f.——Special retreats for organized groups or total membership
g.——Vacation church school
h.——Visitation evangelism
i.——Other————————————————————————————

19. *Evaluate the effectiveness of current program in your church.* (Check *after each type* of activity.)

	Well	Fair	Poor	Don't know
a. Worship	——	——	——	——
b. Christian education	——	——	——	——
c. Fellowship	——	——	——	——
d. Community ministry	——	——	——	——

20. *I wish my church had:* (Check as many as apply.)

a.——Experimental worship
b.——Mid-week service
c.——Church school
d.——A men's group
e.——A social action group
f.——Retreats for church leaders
g.——Graded choirs
h.——A women's group
i. ——A youth group for——ages
j. ——Study groups in homes
k.——Board of committee of
l. ——Other————————————

21. *Christians join churches for many reasons. How important was EACH OF THESE REASONS for you personally when you joined your present church?* (Check one column for each reason.)

	Very important	Somewhat important	Not too important
a. Enjoyed its friendly atmosphere.	——	——	——
b. For the sake of my children	——	——	——
c. A place to serve others	——	——	——
d. Grew up in church school	——	——	——
e. Program appealed to me	——	——	——
f. Invited to join by a member	——	——	——
g. Invited to join by the minister ..	——	——	——
h. Worship service	——	——	——

i. Liked the minister . . . .   ——   ——   ——

j. Liked the people I met in church.   ——   ——   ——

k. Preferred the denomination . . . .   ——   ——   ——

l. Followed example of a friend . .   ——   ——   ——

22. *How necessary do you feel it is for a Christian to believe or do the following?* (Check once after each item.)

	Necessary	Desirable	Not necessary
a. Accept church creeds	——	——	——
b. Be an active church member	——	——	——
c. Attend Sunday worship regularly . . .	——	——	——
d. Believe in Jesus as Savior	——	——	——
e. Have a specific conversion experience	——	——	——
f. Be baptized	——	——	——
g. Obey the Ten Commandments	——	——	——
h. Pray and read the Bible daily	——	——	——
i. Work for social justice	——	——	——
j. Contribute to the church	——	——	——
k. Follow Christ as Lord in daily life . . .	——	——	——

23. *I believe my church and denomination should cooperate with other churches and denominations:* (Check as many as apply.)

a.——Not at all   c. ——At the regional and state level

b.——At the local level   d.——At the national level

24. *As a church member or participant, to what degree are you seeking help or guidance in the following areas of your life?* (Check one after each.)

I want my church to help me . . .	Much	Some	Little
a. Be alert to needs of others in community .	——	——	——
b. Give my children Christian education	——	——	——
c. Find meaning for personal existence	——	——	——
d. Know God's love and care for me	——	——	——
e. Meet my personal problems	——	——	——
f. Strengthen my faith and devotion	——	——	——
g. Understand my work as Christian vocation	——	——	——
h. Work for justice in the community and world	——	——	——
i. Understand the Bible	——	——	——
j. Understand Christian doctrine	——	——	——

k. Use my leisure time more effectively ..... —— —— ——
l. Become trained as an effective lay leader . —— —— ——

25. *Check your opinion as to the category that best describes each statement given below:* (Check once after each item.)

	True	Probably true	Probably not true	Not true
a. All men are born with a sinful nature.	——	——	——	—
b. All men are equal in the sight of God.	——	——	——	—
c. God answers prayer	——	——	——	—
d. God revealed himself to man in Jesus Christ...........................	——	——	——	—
e. Hell is a just punishment for sinners .	——	——	——	—
f. Jesus rose from the dead	——	——	——	—
g. Jesus was born of a virgin.........	——	——	——	—
h. Sin is separation from God	——	——	——	—
i. The Bible is the Word of God	——	——	——	—
j. The Church is the Body of Christ ...	——	——	——	—
k. There is life after death	——	——	——	—
l. We are justified by faith	——	——	——	—

26. *Indicate which of the following church responsibilities you have or have had in the last five years:* (Circle each that you currently have.)

a.——Officer
b.——Board member
c.——Committee member
d.——Church school teacher
e. ——Small group leader
f.——Home visitation
g.——Choir
h.——Usher
i. ——Officer of church organization
j.——Other (specify)————

27. *In your personal life, do you*

a.——Pray at meals?
b.——Read the Bible daily?
c.——Use a devotional book?

28. *Which of the following should be responsibilities for your church?* (Check once after each item.)

	Yes	No	Not sure
a. Teaching the Bible	——	——	——
b. Working for racial justice and equality ..	——	——	——

	Much	Some	Little
c. Helping young people	——	——	——
d. Encouraging personal involvement in community organization	——	——	——
e. Helping people make their occupation Christian	——	——	——
f. Effecting change in government policies	——	——	——
g. Caring for needs of older people	——	——	——
h. Fostering devotional life	——	——	——
i. Supporting world missions	——	——	——

29. *How helpful has your church actually been to you in the following areas of your life?* (Check once after each item.)

In helping me to:	Much	Some	Little
a. Be alert to needs of others in community. .	——	——	——
b. Give my children Christian education	——	——	——
c. Find meaning for personal existence	——	——	——
d. Know God's love and care for me	——	——	——
e. Meet my personal problems	——	——	——
f. Strengthen my faith and devotion	——	——	——
g. Understand my work as Christian vocation	——	——	——
h. Work for justice in community and world .	——	——	——
i. Understand the Bible	——	——	——
j. Understand Christian doctrine	——	——	——
k. Use my leisure time more effectively	——	——	——
l. Become trained as an effective lay leader. .	——	——	——

30. *How long have you been a member of American Baptist congregations?*

a.——Less than 1 year   c.—— 3 to 5 years   e.——10 to 20 years
b.——1 to 3 years   d.—— 5 to 10 years   f.——More than 20

31. *Check below what you consider to be appropriate ways for the church to react to community problems:*

a.——Not be involved directly.
b.——Move no faster than the neighborhood in which it is located.
c.——Deal with the question only in sermons or study groups.
d.——Individuals may work on special projects at their own initiative.
e.——Form special action groups to work on crisis problems.
f.——Lead the community to solve its problems.

32. *Which kinds of cooperative involvements should local churches undertake?*

a.——Joint services of worship
b.——Pastoral exchanges
c.——Interchurch parishes
d.——Joint programs of education

e.——Participate in councils of
churches
f.——Participate in community better-
ment efforts
g.——Other (Specify)

33. *In the area of public affairs, how important are the following:* (Number
the THREE most important 1, 2, 3.)

a.——Quality public education
b.——Highway safety
c.——Meaningful leisure
d.——Respect for authority
e.——Adequate jobs
f. ——Criminal justice and penal reform
g.——Achieving world peace
h.——Quality housing
i. ——Environmental quality
j. ——Welfare reform
k.——Quality health care
l. ——Police protection for my family
m.——A trustworthy government
n.——Achieving racial justice
o.——Solution to the drug and alcohol problem
p.——Pride in America
q.——Other (Specify) ———————————————————

NOTE: The following questions refer to the Pittsburgh Baptist Association.

34. *What involvements do you have in the Association?* (Check all that
apply.)

a.——Association officer
b.——Association board of
directors
c. ——Association department
d.——Association committee

e.——Association delegate
f.——Past member of Association
board of directors, department,
or committee
g.——Other

h.——None

35. *As far as you are concerned, how important are the following Association programs?* (Number the THREE most important 1, 2, 3.)

206

a. ——Evangelism
b.——New church development
c. ——Christian education
d.——Camping
e. ——Youth work
f. ——Men's work
g. ——Women's work
h.——Campus ministry
i. ——Neighborhood ministries

j. ——Continuing education for pastors
k. ——Pastoral placement
l. ——Promotion of world mission support
m.——Stewardship training
n. ——Ecumenical relations
o. ——Care for the elderly
p. ——Black-white relations
q. ——Other (Specify)

36. *How well do you feel the Association is serving in the following areas?* (Check once after each.)

	Well	Fair	Poor	Don't know
a. Evangelism	——	——	——	——
b. New church development	——	——	——	——
c. Christian education	——	——	——	——
d. Camping	——	——	——	——
e. Youth Work	——	——	——	——
f. Men's work	——	——	——	——
g. Women's work	——	——	——	——
h. Campus ministry	——	——	——	——
i. Neighborhood ministries	——	——	——	——
j. Continuing education for pastors	——	——	——	——
k. Pastoral placement	——	——	——	——
l. Promotion of world mission support	——	——	——	——
m. Stewardship training	——	——	——	——
n. Ecumenical relations	——	——	——	——
o. Care for the elderly	——	——	——	——
p. Black-white relations	——	——	——	——
q. Other (Specify)	——	——	——	——

37. *Which of the following do you think are the most pressing needs of the Pittsburgh Baptist Association?* (Number the THREE most pressing 1, 2, 3.)

a.——Increased funding	j. ——More interdenominational cooperation
b.——More staff	
c.——Greater staff efficiency	k.——More involvement with urban issues
d.——More lay participation	
e.——More factfinding and planning	l. ——More involvement in higher education
f.——Establish more churches	m.——Better Christian education services
g.——Determine priorities	
h.——Seek membership gains	n. ——More effective evangelism
i. ——More promotion of world missions	o. ——More effective communication with churches
	p. ——More programs for spiritual growth
	q. ——More experimental ministries

38. *Who in the Pittsburgh Baptist Association do you think establishes policy?*

a.——The Association board of directors	e.——The executive committee
	f. ——The congregations
b.——The delegates in annual meetings	g.——The pastors
	h.——I do not know who establishes policy
c.——The staff	
d.——A combination of (name which ones _____)	i. ——Other (Name)

Note: If you think policy is not now established by the right group, who do you think should establish policy for the Association?

_____

39. *What should the Association do?* (Check all that apply.)

a.——Help congregations serve more effectively, *only when they ask for help.*

b.——Initiate contacts with local congregations and provide resources.

c.——Provide a means by which congregations can serve a larger mission.

d.——Undertake experimental ministries to research new ways of serving.

e.——Start and maintain specialized ministries.

f.——Encourage and help congregations start specialized ministries.

g.——Pool resources from the congregations for support of weaker churches.

h.——Take stands on social issues.

i. ——Engage in interdenominational church extension.

j. ——Be a channel between congregations and the American Baptist Churches in the USA.

k.——Other (Specify)

l. ——I have no opinion.

40. In 1968 a proposal to merge the Pittsburgh Baptist Association, Pennsylvania Baptist Convention, Delaware Baptist Convention, and Philadelphia Baptist Association was turned down. The boards of directors of these four administrative units then approved a Covenant Relationship with a committee to develop certain cooperative ministries. A prime example is the area ministry in which the Pittsburgh Baptist Association has shared its staff so far as time has permitted with Baptist churches in three surrounding associations. The Covenant Committee is authorized to function through December, 1975.

In light of your present understanding: (Please select one.)

The Pittsburgh Baptist Association should focus its ministry and program primarily upon serving its present 60 member churches, after the commitment to the Covenant Relationship runs out in 1975.

The Pittsburgh Baptist Association should participate with other administrative units, and the Baptist churches in a surrounding area, in developing a new organizational structure with staff and financial support committed to serving directly the larger number of churches.

41. *Please add anything you would like to say to the consultant team about the study.*

_____

_____

_____

_____

_____

209

Please return your completed questionnaire in the enclosed envelope. Thank you,

Strategy Study Committee

EXHIBIT 10-B

INVENTORY OF PRINTED RESOURCES
ON HAND FOR THE PITTSBURGH STUDY

REGIONAL RESOURCES

Department of Community Affairs Programs (nd)

Dimensions of Year 2000: A Basis for Plan Preparation in Southwestern Pennsylvania (4/73)

Poverty in Southwestern Pennsylvania (nd)

Toward a Regional Plan: Development Policies for the Next 30 Years (1/70)

Historical Analysis of the Southwestern Pennsylvania Region (9/67)

Issues in a Region of Contrasts (11/68)

Pennsylvania School District and Intermediate Unit Directory (7/71)

Cooperative Extension Service 1971-72 Program Year: Purpose, Financing, Accomplishments (1/72)

Population Projections County by County for the State through 1990

Selected Measures of Economic Development for 67 Pennsylvania Counties

Steelworker's Program of Education and Action in Kokomo (1/70)

Steel Labor (4/73: 5/73)

ALLEGHENY COUNTY

Development Districts and Population by Each District through 1976

50 Years: Health and Welfare Association of Allegheny County (1972)

Report of the Reappraisal and Development Commission: New Directions for the Seventies (1972)

Report to the Housing Inadequacies Task Force (5/71)

Report of the Task Force for the Chronically Unemployed (7/71)

Cause for Concern: Report of the Task Force on Youth Problems (12/71)

Report of the Task Force on Services to Families and Children (11/71)

Report of the Health Task Force (11/71)

Allegheny County Parks brochures

Text for Slide Presentation: Department of Parks, Recreation and Conservation

Allegheny County Board of Assistance case count by census tract (3/73)

Allegheny County Board of Assistance caseload from 1945 to 1970

Allegheny County Board of Assistance monthly average number of persons on public assistance 1960 to 1973

Allegheny County Mental Health and Mental Retardation Goals Statement (5/73)
Allegheny County MH and MR Catchment areas (11/72)
County-wide Agencies related to the MH and MR department (nd)
Allegheny County Health Department Services Directory (nd)
Allegheny County Health Department Annual Reports for 1971 and 1972
Building a Healthier Community: Allegheny County Health Department 1957-1967

FAYETTE COUNTY

A Blueprint for Fayette County's Future (7/69)

FAYETTE-GREENE-WASHINGTON COUNTIES

Directory 1972-73 Intermediate Unit 1
Brochure describing Intermediate Unit 1 (nd)
Intermediate Unit 1 News (5/72 through 5/73)

GREENE COUNTY

Solid Waste Management Plan (nd)
Digest Report: Comprehensive Plan (1973)

INDIANA COUNTY

Population Study and Projections (1/68)
Summary Comprehensive Plan (10/67)

WASHINGTON COUNTY

Economic Analysis of Washington County (1971)

WESTMORELAND COUNTY

Annual Directory 1972-73 Intermediate Unit VII
Proposed Plan for Community College of Westmoreland County (12/69)
Brochure about Westmoreland County

PITTSBURGH

Report of juvenile offenses 1966 through 1971
Report of arrests for drug offenses by age and type of drug 1967-1971
Guidelines for Planning: YMCA (2/65)
YMCA of Pittsburgh: 1972 Annual Report
The Impact of the University of Pittsburgh on the Local Economy (4/72)

MT. LEBANON

Fact Sheet—1973 on Mount Lebanon Township

Mt. Lebanon Jaycees Community Attitude Survey (2/72)
Mt. Lebanon School District Facts and Figures 1972-73
Mt. Lebanon Facts for Voters 1973

RELIGIOUS

Selected statistics and interpretive documents from Christian Associates
Directory of Office of Education, Diocese of Greensburgh 1972-73

8/8/73

XI

Some Guiding Principles

We are apt to believe what is pleasant rather than what is true.

William Penn

Resolving conflict is a problem in any organization. It can be especially difficult in a voluntary fellowship such as a church. The old adage "An ounce of prevention is worth a pound of cure" was never more applicable than it is to the church. A pastor who knows how to work through lay people can practice the prevention necessary. Lay people who understand their responsibility to work with and help the pastor maintain effectiveness should understand this, too. The pastor should develop a relationship with a few lay leaders that permits him to explore his ideas with them, develop them, or abandon them. As for those that should be pursued, he should let a lay person carry the ball with the congregation. Otherwise, he can expect to alienate a few people with each idea; and if he has many ideas, then it will not take long to get the majority against him. There is a saying sometimes seen on desks or office walls—"There is no limit to what can be accomplished if one doesn't care who gets the credit." The pastor of a growing, a successful church is automatically going to reap a lot of credit if alienation is avoided. This is not suggesting compromise of principle, just good management. When conflict does arise, try this:

1. Try to see the issues from each point of view.
2. Then ask each participant to think only of those things on

which there is agreement. In other words, divide the problem into pieces. Usually you will find that there is agreement on most pieces of the problem. People who have much in common certainly should be able to resolve the little piece remaining and usually will.

In the business world, there is a saying, "To sell John Smith what John Smith buys, you must see John Smith through John Smith's eyes." In church, and perhaps business, too, it is better to change that to "see John Smith through God's eyes."

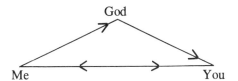

Instead of looking across from me to you through my eyes, which are fogged by both my faults and your faults, ask God, the Creator of both, to help me to see you as He sees you. My vision immediately improves and problems tend to disappear.

When should a church change pastors? When it is best for the church and best for him, it is best to move on. One should be alert to these signs.

1. When the pastor makes a habit of delivering replies to individuals or small groups in his messages from the pulpit.

2. When either pastor or people are unable to accept people where they are as a starting point.

3. When the pastor makes frequent use of labels to categorize a group of people as he sees one or two, instead of recognizing individual human beings. In lecturing to college students who tend to do this, this illustration has been found useful:

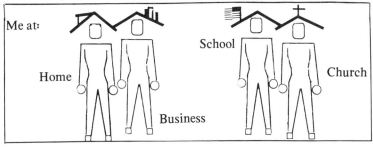

Within a twenty-four hour span, I may be under the roof of my home as a husband and father, a business corporation as an executive, of the university as a lecturer, and of the church as a worshiper and worker. I will be the same flesh and blood and bones with essentially the same motivation with minor deviations. If I am not what I should be as a businessman, do not blame my boss or something called business. Yes, the boss and my associates can have some influence; but my home, church, and school are the places where I have really become what I am. Perhaps if the church did its job, the home and other institutions would also be more effective; and a lot of name-calling could be avoided.

4. When the pastor ceases to be stimulated by the challenge of leadership of a people. This shows up in many ways. A pastor starts searching for committees, organizations, and any other activities to consume his time and avoid boredom. This pastor's church is probably inactive and not growing. A pastor once spoke with me about consulting with business corporations on human relations. His ministry in past years had received acclaim. Much growth had taken place, but it had not kept pace with the community. He had become bored with the need to keep certain functions going on a repetitive basis and had eased off. To his credit, this soon became apparent to him, and he resigned to make a change. Both pastor and church were soon functioning better as a result of the change.

5. When a significant number of members cease to believe or act as though they agree with or support the pastor's leadership. Never mind whose fault it is—change is desirable, and every effort should be made in a Christian way to help each other wake up to whatever the problems and opportunities may be.

6. When age or health prevent doing the job. We are not suggesting that a people abandon the needs or welfare of their pastor; but, if proper plans for pension and health care benefits have been made on the part of the pastor and the church, it should be possible to adequately care for the needs of the retired pastor and the pastoral needs of the church through another pastor. The following letter is one example of a very wise pastor acting under these circumstances.

Dear Folks:

Last October the announcement was made to the church that I would retire April 1.

When the date arrived and you hadn't chosen a pastor, it seemed that it would be helpful for me to continue until you did. I realize now that this brings about a period of suspense and uncertainty. Many have expressed a desire to have this arrangement continue indefinitely. With this in mind, you are just naturally not ready to choose a successor.

We all want what is best for the church and for the work of the Kingdom. It is absolutely essential that we have unity. Therefore you will kindly consider my resignation as taking effect by September 1, 1961.

In choosing a new pastor, remember that he will do many things differently and it will take adjusting on your part as well as his. Pray that God will direct in the choosing of a man and that all may have a loving spirit, even when opinions differ. I know that you are mature enough and Christian enough to do this.

Lovingly,
Your Pastor

Note that this pastor had at first tried to retire and then had helped out by staying on until a successor was found. This became a divisive force, because some members would not consider anyone else as long as their pastor of fifteen years was in the pulpit week after week and others wanted to get on with the job that had to be done. Also, loyalties built up over the years to one man will prevent some potential pastors from accepting the invitation to serve. The church needs unity, and divided loyalties do not help. So, pastor, plan, if possible, to be unavailable to your old parish when you retire; and, lay people, when the time to retire is at hand, help your pastor through it—do not delay it. I have seen people become dishonest under these circumstances. A pastor, sensing a change is needed, puts out a feeler by saying, "I think maybe the time has come for me to make a change and move on." Immediately, someone, who knows this is the right thing, emotionally blurts out, "Oh, no! You can't do that!"

Leaders do not *react* they *act*! They do not wait for the future; they make the future! Lay people and pastors, together with God's Spirit leading, can do just this—be *leaders*. And it helps a lot if pastor and individual lay people spend time regularly talking together about the Lord's business—the church.

Too many church situations remind me of the story of the older man and his wife who were driving along in a buggy. The wife, after an extended period of silence, said, "Dear, wouldn't it be wonderful if we could always pull together like the two horses?" The husband's short reply was, "We could if there were only one tongue between us, like them."

We can act and speak as if with one tongue if we have planned and worked together as leaders should.

There are many able, responsible lay people desirous of serving Our Lord. Positive leadership to get them involved, to utilize the varied talents that have given them success in other fields, will make that same talent available to the church. I have seen them "turned off" by the church's leadership. I hope to see them "turned on" again for the good of mankind, the church, and the Glory of God. It can be done.